Now You See It, Now You Don't

Now You See It, Now You Don't

Biblical Perspectives on the Relationship between Magic and Religion

SHAWNA DOLANSKY

Winona Lake, Indiana
EISENBRAUNS
2008

Published for Pryor Pettengill Publishers
by Eisenbrauns
P.O. Box 275
Winona Lake, IN 46590

www.eisenbrauns.com

Library of Congress Cataloging-in-Publication Data

Dolansky, Shawna
  Now you see it, now you don't : biblical perspectives on the relationship
  between magic and religion / by Shawna Dolansky.
    p. cm.
  Includes bibliographical references.
  ISBN 978-1-57506-805-3 (hardcover : alk. paper)
    1. Magic—Biblical teaching. 2. Magic, Ancient. 3. Bible, O.T.—
  Criticism, interpretation, etc. 4. Magic—Religious aspects—Judaism.
  I. Title.
  BS680.M3D65   2008
  221.8′13343—dc22

                                   2008044576

Table of Contents

Abbreviations

ANET	*Ancient Near Eastern Texts Relating to the Old Testament* (3d ed,; ed. J. B. Pritchard; Princeton: Princeton University Press, 1969)
ANRW	*Aufstieg und Niedergang der romischen Welt: Geschichte und Kultur Roms im Spiegel der neueren Forschung* (ed. H. Temporini and W. Haase; Berlin: 1972-)
ARM	Archives royales de Mari
BASOR	*Bulletin of the American Schools of Oriental Research*
BDB	F. Brown, S. R. Driver, and C. A. Briggs, *Hebrew and English Lexicon of the Old Testament* (Oxford: Clarendon, 1953)
BZAW	Beiheft zur ZAW
CAD	*The Assyrian Dictionary of the Oriental Institute of the University of Chicago* (ed. A. L. Oppenheim et al.; Chicago: The Oriental Institute of the University of Chicago, 1956-)
CBQ	*Catholic Biblical Quarterly*
HSM	Harvard Semitic Monographs
HUCA	*Hebrew Union College Annual*
JANES	*Journal of the Ancient Near Eastern Society*
JAOS	*Journal of the American Oriental Society*
JBL	*Journal of Biblical Literature*
JHS	*Journal of Hellenic Studies*
JNES	*Journal of Near Eastern Studies*
JSOT	*Journal for the Study of the Old Testament*
JSOTSup	Journal for the Study of the Old Testament Supplement Series
UF	*Ugarit-Forschungen*
VAB	Vorderasiatische Bibliothek
VT	*Vetus Testamentum*
ZAW	*Zeitschrift fur die Alttestamentliche Wissenschaft*

Introduction

Separating Religion from Magic in Biblical Scholarship

Religion and Magic

> *For if I had been there then, should I not have thought, from the fact that the magicians did like things to those which Moses did, either that Moses was a magician, or that the magicians wrought their signs by divine commission? For I should not have thought it likely that the same things could be effected by magicians, even in appearance, which he who was sent by God performed.*[1]

In other words, how can we tell the difference between magic and religion if the end result appears to be the same? This is an important question in Western theology, as "magic" traditionally carries a negative connotation in religious contexts. But how can we condemn magic if Moses is one of its strongest champions? The solution has long been a matter of semantics: because Moses' actions were sanctioned by God, they were religious (miraculous) and not magical. Not a very satisfying response; the uneasy feeling remains that Moses and the Egyptian *magicians* performed the exact same "miracles."

The problem of differentiating between actions that are magical and those that are religious is important in the fields of anthropology and religious studies. Both magic and religion claim access to realms outside of ordinary reality and attempt to manipulate supernatural forces for desired outcomes in the natural world. Scholars have approached the categories of magic and religion from a variety of perspectives, distinguishing them on the basis of their techniques, social effects, and the status of their chief proponents. Some have suggested that there is no real difference, that the categories merely denote social conventions ("what I do is religion, what you do is magic") and that the terms themselves should be dissolved altogether. At first glance, this seems a fair (and easy) solution to the problem posed above. Yet when you pick up a book on the topic of magic in the ancient world, you *do* have a different expectation of what you will be learning than if you were to explore the field of *religion* in the ancient world. You would expect them to overlap, perhaps to a great extent, but you

---

[1] "Clementine Recognitions," 3.57; trans. T. Smith, in *The Ante-Nicene Fathers*, vol. 8 (New York: Charles Scribner's Sons, 1903).

would still retain a sense that there is some substantive, and not merely semantic, difference.

A discussion of "magic in the Hebrew Bible" must first propose, and then arduously defend, a definition of "magic" in order to validate the subsequent categorization of acts and behaviors under scrutiny. Many critics would undermine such an effort at the very outset, denying altogether the possibility of a substantive definition of the term "magic." Yet, despite the reluctance of many scholars to offer a qualitative definition of magic, the very existence of their scholarship on the subject suggests that at some level they do have a sense of distinct behaviors, practices, activities, rituals and objects that can be categorized as distinctly "magical." Here is the irony: there is no question that if a seminar or conference is calling for papers on the subject of "magic," scholars will have a sense of what kind of research is being solicited. Intuitively, we all know what is meant by the term "magic." The problems arise when we try to classify particular behavior as either "magical" or "religious," particularly when we try to generalize such categories across space and time.

This problem is only as modern as the categories themselves. I suggested above that both magic and religion claim access to realms outside of ordinary reality and attempt to manipulate supernatural forces for desired outcomes in the natural world. However, it can be argued that the distinction between "natural" and "supernatural" itself is very much a modern scientific one that has little relevance in ancient or pre-industrialized societies. In some parts of the ancient world, as in many present-day "primitive" societies, there is evidence that the practitioners of activities that we would label "magical" or "religious," made no distinction between "magic" and "religion." The authors of the Bible, for example, may not have: the fact that Aaron could turn a rod into a snake was impressive, yet Egyptian magicians managed the same feat. And the biblical author of this story seems to have no problem with this! Whether the God of Israel or the gods of Egypt were the source of the magicians' power is not relevant for the author. The fact that Moses and Aaron demonstrated their authority, at least at first, by the use of tricks with which Egyptian magicians were familiar, does not diminish their status in the author's eyes, and presumably would not in the eyes of the intended audience either. And yet the Deuteronomic Law Code strictly prohibits such activities in Israel, not for lack of efficacy but rather because they were abhorrent to Yahweh (Deut 18:12).

For scholars then, the real problem is how to legitimately apply our own categories, and our modern definitions of those categories, to ancient phenomena. Do such categories make sense for the ancient world? When archaeologists and paleoanthropologists examine the cave paintings of ancient Europe, they do not classify them as either "religious" or "magical"; the assumption is that so far back in history, there was no difference between the two. However, by the time of classical Greece, Athenian literature shows that the Greeks themselves did differentiate between magic and religion (although they do not always agree on what that difference is). At what juncture then, in the history of human cultures, can we begin to see the difference and legitimately apply these current labels? And more to the point of the present work, what about biblical Israel?

In the contemporary Western world, we understand religion as a belief in supernatural powers resulting in behaviors that attempt to cultivate a propitiatory relationship with those powers. Usually such behaviors are imbued with moral overtones; from the perspective of a practitioner, religion helps an individual to become morally "good" (the definition of "good," however, may vary from religion to religion). Religion can be an intensely personal feeling or individual relationship with the supernatural. We begin to differentiate "religion" from "magic" in the historical record with the increasing complexity of society. What historians and anthropologists call religion has its origins in society, societal needs, and social expression. The priest as religious leader arose as a consequence of the demands of social and economic conditions such as agriculture and organized political leadership.[2]

What distinguishes magic from religion, and the practitioners of magic from priests, is that magic is practiced outside of considerations of moral boundaries, and is defined by *actions* that are supernatural, either in origin or in their intended consequences. Magical practitioners offer constant proof of their link with the supernatural, whereas priests merely maintain the tenets of belief to guide their followers in the proper rituals and behaviors. Aside from questions of morality, "Magic and religion differ then in two ways: in the degree of personalization of power, and in the question of who has the power. The magician has mana and personally controls the impersonal world .... By contrast, the religionist worries for his soul, feels his helplessness, and dependently implores an external Anima to use its power on his behalf."[3] It is easy to see where the two categories overlap: "Both shaman and priest lay claim to omnipotence or the manipulation of it."[4] However, while priests maintain belief and tradition, magicians inspire belief by their ability to offer tangible proof of the supernatural. Historically, as societies became more complex, priests and shamans first coexisted, and then gradually priests began replacing shamans as religious leaders, marginalizing shamanic magical practices and offering priestly knowledge

---

[2] M. J. Winkelman, *Shamans, Priests and Witches: A Cross-Cultural Study of Magico-Religious Practitioners* (Arizona State University, Anthropological Research Papers No. 44: 1992), pp. 125-6.

[3] Weston LaBarre, *The Ghost Dance. Origins of Religion* (Illinois: Waveland Press Inc., 1990) p. 372.

[4] LaBarre, *The Ghost Dance*, p. 375.

and ritual as the only means for the common person to communicate with and relate to the supernatural.[5]

Biblical Scholarship

In Exodus 7 through 9, Egyptian magicians and sorcerers perform the same wonders as Moses and Aaron. Does this make Moses and Aaron "magicians" or the acts they perform "magic" by definition? What about other acts of magic in the Bible, such as Jacob's genetic manipulations with rods and sheep (Gen 30:35-43), Elijah's creation of a bottomless jar of flour and jug of oil (1 Kings 17:16), or Elisha's purification of polluted water (2 Kings 2:21)? In the face of the explicit prohibition of magic and divination in Deuteronomy 18, the biblical attitude toward magic and its relationship with Israelite religion is confusing. This is compounded by traditional interpretations of the text that infer theological distinctions between the divinely inspired acts of God's agents (e.g. Moses) and others (magicians) for whom the prohibitions are actually intended.

The issue is further complicated by the implications of finding magic in Israelite religion, both from a modern theological point of view, and with respect to the issue of monotheism in ancient Israel. Some scholars, associating "magic" with "pagan" and wishing to maintain the uniqueness of Israel from its neighbors, emphatically deny the existence, or at least the legitimacy, of magic within Israelite religion. This view is fostered by the Deuteronomic Law Code's strong prohibition of magical practices and practitioners. G. von Rad represents this perspective with his emphasis on the lack of magic within the religion of ancient Israel: "Its absence already gives the Israel of the time an exceptional position within all the fairly comparable forms in the history of religion .... We explain as deriving from the peculiar nature of Yahwism the limit here set to magic and its competency. Yahweh's invasive power, revealing himself on all sides as personal will, was absolutely incompatible with the impersonal automatic action of the forces of magic."[6]

Y. Kaufmann took the issue of Israel's uniqueness much further; his work on ancient Israelite religion repeatedly emphasizes the differences between the pagan religion of Israel's neighbors and that portrayed in the Hebrew Bible.[7] For Kauf-

---

[5] See further, *Shamanism, History and the State*, eds. N. Thomas and C. Humphrey (Ann Arbor: University of Michigan Press, 1996).

[6] G. von Rad, *Old Testament Theology*, vol. 1, trans. D. M. G. Stalker (Edinburgh/ London: Oliver and Boyd, 1962), p. 34f.

[7] Y. Kaufmann, *Toledot ha'emunah hayisra'elit* (Tel Aviv: Bialik Institute-Dvir), Vols. 1-7 (1937-1948). Translated and abridged from the Hebrew by M. Greenberg as *The Religion of Israel* (Chicago: University of Chicago Press, 1960). Citations and references herein refer to Greenberg's translation.

mann, the difference is not simply a matter of polytheism vs. monotheism. Rather, Kaufmann argues that pagan thought presupposes a "metadivine realm" beyond even the gods themselves, from which the gods appropriate their power. Human magic is an attempt to imitate the gods in trying to control the cosmos. The stories told about the gods' strivings with humans and with the metadivine realm comprise pagan mythology. Thus myth and magic intertwine in pagan systems, whereas both are almost completely absent in biblical Israel.[8] According to Kaufmann, another element of pagan religion that sets Israelite religion apart is the notion of cosmic dualism in which impurity is regarded as a demonic, evil force feared even by the gods. The monotheism of Israel, Kaufmann argued, precludes the existence of anything beyond Yahweh; thus even the forces of evil derive from God, as there cannot be a belief in demonic forces.[9] With no metadivine realm and all power in the hands of one God, there can also be no magic, although remnants of Israel's pagan past survive in transmuted form.[10] For Kaufmann, in the Hebrew Bible history and monotheism replace mythology and magic.[11]

Kaufmann's and Von Rad's claims that magic is absent in ancient Israel can be maintained only if the actions of such figures as Moses, Elijah, and Elisha are classified as something other than magic. Yet in any other context, ancient or modern, such acts as transmutation of rods into snakes or causing an ax-head to float would be termed "magical" without a second thought. Von Rad's statement describing the forces of magic as "impersonal automatic action" hint that his idea of what constitutes magic is something very separate from, and inferior to, religion.

And yet there are some major differences between the religion described in the Hebrew Bible and that of Israel's neighbors. Part of Kaufmann's contrastive evidence refers to the absence of incantations by Israelite priests against evil forces, as compared to the Mesopotamian *āšipu* for whom *šiptu* (incantation) was prominent.[12] Other scholars have noted the lack of incantatory material in the Bible as a definite point of difference from the abundance of Mesopotamian and Egyptian magical texts that have survived, and have drawn a variety of conclusions from this absence.[13] B. Levine claims, "Israel has no need for omens, since it has the benefit of prophecy," but points out that "Therapeutic magic is never prohibited. On the

---

[8] Kaufmann, *Toledot ha'emunah hayisra'elit*, pp. 22-24.

[9] Kaufmann, *Toledot ha'emunah hayisra'elit*, pp. 60-66.

[10] Kaufmann, *Toledot ha'emunah hayisra'elit*, pp. 80-115; and see our discussion in Chapter Four.

[11] Kaufmann, *Toledot ha'emunah hayisra'elit*, pp. 78-80.

[12] Kaufmann, *Toledot ha'emunah hayisra'elit*, p. 106.

[13] See, for example, H. C. Brichto, *The Problem of 'Curse' in the Hebrew Bible* (JBL Monograph Series 13:1963); and B. Levine, *In the Presence of the Lord* (Leiden: E. J. Brill, 1974).

contrary: it was employed by priests and men of God."[14] H. C. Brichto states that references to magical pronouncements in biblical literature are more of a substratum than a reflection of actual texts in use for magical purposes.[15] We will examine such claims and our own conclusions with respect to the absence of magical texts in the Bible, in Chapter Two.

In addition to the lack of incantations in the Bible, another major point of departure for biblical scholars has been the lists of prohibited activities relating to magic and divination in legal texts. In the nineteenth century, W. Robertson Smith[16] examined the forms of magic listed in Deut 18:10-11, agreeing with traditional scholarship that these practices were foreign to Israelite religion but cautioning that such syncretism as was implied here could have occurred only if there were already underlying commonalities between Israelite and Canaanite religions. Like von Rad, his focus on the prohibitions of Deuteronomy 18 led Robertson Smith to conclude that in ancient Israel magic was an illegal pagan concept, connected with the worship of foreign gods. However, he further noted both "the use of many base superstitions in nominal connection with Jehovah-worship" and the fact that practices forbidden by Deuteronomy 18 appear to have been legitimate in older writings (JE, for example). In the end, however, Robertson Smith characterized magic as "an isolated erratic phenomenon" in ancient Israel. Such a view not only presumes an essential difference between (proper) religion and ("superstitious") magic, a questionable assumption, but asserts that magic is alien to Israelite religion, an illegal import. Yet there is evidence throughout the Bible that magic is not superimposed on a pristine Israelite religion but rather is present at the foundation of the religion and instrumental throughout its history. Robertson Smith's observation about the different perspectives of diverse authors, however, is an insightful point of departure for the present study.

T. W. Davies wrote the first comprehensive scholarly work on the subject of magic in ancient Israel.[17] Influenced by nineteenth century evolutionary schemes, Davies concluded that magic belonged to a polytheistic stage in the development of the religion of Israel and that magic in the Bible represents both a low form of biblical religion that preceded the full realization of monotheism, and a degeneration or retreat from monotheism when it appears alongside it. More modern studies of biblical magic also separate magic from religion as a distinct and less sophisticated

---

[14] Levine, pp. 89-90.

[15] Brichto, *The Problem of 'Curse' in the Hebrew*, pp. 205ff.

[16] W. Robertson Smith, "On the Forms of Divination and Magic Enumerated in Deut 18:10-11," *Journal of Philology* 13 (1884), pp. 273-287 and 14 (1885), pp. 112-128.

[17] T. W. Davies, *Magic, Divination and Demonology Among the Hebrews and their Neighbours* (London: J. Clarke and Co., 1898).

social behavior. H. Wheeler Robinson[18] and J. Lindblom[19] considered magic in relation to prophecy, and both emphasized the differences between the "magical" (coercive behavior of the individual) and the "religious" (submission to the will and power of Yahweh).[20] It is this kind of negative judgment of magic in relation to religion that has led some contemporary scholars to reject the categories outright. It is difficult to see, for example, how changing a rod into a snake constitutes "coercive" as opposed to "submissive" behavior; it seems such judgmental categorization applies only from an outsider's perspective.

Only fairly recently has more work devoted to the place of magic in ancient Israel begun to appear. Other than several dissertations and monographs,[21] such scholarship either takes the form of articles on questions of definition that employ a handful of examples of the use of magic in the Hebrew Bible, or discuss a story or an object that seems "magical." Most scholars define magic according to their own interpretations of specific biblical incidents rather than attempting a general categorization of acts that can be classified as "magic." For example, J. Neusner treats the plague narratives in Exodus as unitary to conclude that although there is no intrinsic difference between Israelite magic ("religion") and Egyptian magic, "the extrinsic difference is God's sponsorship of the former, the demonic character of the latter, or, in secular terms, one is ours, the other is theirs, and that without regard to whether we deal with knowledge or action. The distinction is systemic, and the difference is social and conventional."[22] Neusner seems to have an intuitive, general sense of what types of acts constitute "magic" but resists defining the term substantively. Like scholars before him, Neusner operates from the premise that there

---

[18] H. Wheeler Robinson, *Inspiration and Revelation in the Old Testament* (Oxford: Blackwell, 1978).

[19] J. Lindblom, *Prophecy in Ancient Israel* (Oxford: Blackwell, 1965).

[20] For related works with similar conclusions see also A. Guillaume, *Prophecy and Divination among the Hebrews and Other Semites* (London: Hodder and Stoughton, 1938), and G. Fohrer, "Prophetie und Magie," *ZAW* 78 (1966) pp. 25-47. Fohrer distinguishes between the magical roots of the symbolic action of the prophet, and the actual utterance which expresses Yahweh's power.

[21] See A. Jeffers, *Magic and Divination in Ancient Palestine and Syria* (Leiden: Brill, 1996); F. Cryer, *Divination in Ancient Israel and its Near Eastern Environment* (*JSOT Sup*: Sheffield, 1994); R. M. Braman, "The Problem of Magic in Ancient Israel: A Century of Studies" (Ph.D. Diss.: Drew University, 1989); J. K. Kuemmerlin-McLean, "Divination and magic in the Religion of Ancient Israel: A Study in Perspectives and Methodology" (Ph.D. Diss.: Vanderbilt University, 1986) and M. Fishbane, "Studies in Biblical Magic: Origins, Uses and Transformations of Terminology and Literary Form" (Ph.D. Diss.: Brandeis, 1971).

[22] J. Neusner, "Science and Magic, Miracle and Magic in Formative Judaism: The System and the Difference," in *Religion, Science and Magic In Concert and in Conflict*, eds. J. Neusner, E. S. Frerichs, P. V. McCracken Flesher (New York: Oxford University Press, 1989), p. 74.

is a difference between magic and religion (or "miracle") and concludes that "Israelite and gentile magicians practice the same magic, but one can differentiate the one from the other. Israelite and gentile sages know the same thing, which is to say, both derive their knowledge from God .... The difference lies in God's differentiation between Israelite miracle and gentile magic."[23]

This type of definition, attempting to present or explain a phenomenon from the point of view of the practitioners, is known in anthropological terminology as an "emic" approach. In an emic perspective, "definitions, distinctions, and values are derived from the actors themselves rather than imposed on them by the observer."[24] When an anthropologist lives with the community under study, he or she tries to see the world from the perspective of the natives to produce an emic description of life in that community. The opposite of this is an etic perspective, an outsider's point of view that uses concepts and categories familiar to the observer to explain other societies, which may have very little meaning to those under observation.

Like Neusner, S. Ricks[25] emphasizes an emic approach to defining magic in the Bible and maintains a distinction between pure religion (Israelite) and magic (pagan): "'magic' ... is quintessentially the activity of the 'outsider' in the Bible." Ricks agrees with Neusner that the decisive difference between the "magician" and men like Moses and Elijah is that Israelites use the power of Yahweh, and this is what makes them both superior and legitimate. The term "magic," then, is not a substantive one but rather a social category: "[I]t is not the nature of the action itself, but the conformity of the action (or actor) to, or deviation from, the values of Israelite society."[26] Both object to any attempt to separate "magic" from "religion" based on a qualitative definition of magic; the distinction is entirely social ("what my side does is a miracle ... what your side does is magic"[27]). Ricks concludes: "Where religion ends and magic begins on the religion-magic continuum depends upon the stance of the person speaking or writing, since it is not possible to divide religion and magic on the basis of any objective set of criteria."[28]

---

[23] J. Neusner, *Religion, Science and Magic In Concert and in Conflict*, p. 76.

[24] D. E. Aune, "Magic in Early Christianity," *ANRW* II 23.2 (1980), p. 1510, n. 4.

[25] S. D. Ricks, "The Magician as Outsider in the Hebrew Bible and the New Testament," in *Ancient Magic and Ritual Power*, eds. M. Meyer and P. Mirecki (Leiden: Brill, 1995) pp. 131-144.

[26] Ricks, *Ancient Magic and Ritual Power*, p. 131.

[27] Neusner, *Religion, Science and Magic In Concert and in Conflict*, p. 61.

[28] Ricks, *Ancient Magic and Ritual Power*, p. 143.

Neusner and Ricks disagree, however, on what the "implicit" (emic) criteria are in the Bible for distinguishing between magic and miracle, demonstrating the ultimate deficiencies of a purely emic approach: in order to be explained in an intelligible fashion to outsiders, the phenomenon must be interpreted in terms that outsiders can understand. As soon as this interpretation takes place, the perspective can no longer legitimately claim insider status. Etic categorization is a necessity if scholarly discourse is to be possible.

Neusner states that both the Egyptian magicians and Moses derive their power from God, and he concludes therefore that it is God's distinction (implicit in the fact that Moses' power is ultimately more effective) that makes the difference. Ricks' conclusion is that what makes Moses' power "religious" and the Egyptians' "magical" is "the perceived power by which the action is performed. Acts performed by the power of Israel's God are, in the view of the writers of the Bible, by that very fact nonmagical, even where they may be formally indistinguishable from those that are depicted as magical."[29] On the other hand, Neusner assumes that the view of the writers is monotheistic, and therefore only God *could* be the sponsor of both actions: the difference is that God makes the Israelites' more effective. Ricks works from the premise that the Egyptians are appealing to their gods, who, from the perspective of the biblical authors, are inferior to Israel's God, and that this is what differentiates between what is miracle and what is magic.

These very different points of departure by two scholars employing similar methods of approach illustrate the problem with a purely emic perspective, particularly where the Bible is concerned: we do not have enough data to approach the subject entirely from an insider's point of view. In the Exodus 7-9 narratives upon which both authors focus, we simply do not know what separates the Egyptian magicians' acts from those of Moses and Aaron. We know that Moses and Aaron prove ultimately more powerful, and that one of the points of the story is a demonstration of Yahweh's power to the Egyptians through these acts. We also know that the Egyptians are called "magicians," and Moses and Aaron are not. But the facts are that qualitatively (etically) they can perform some of the same actions, and these kinds of actions can substantively (and not just socially) be termed "magical" both from the point of view of the authors (who call the Egyptians "magicians") as well as from a more objective standpoint. This indicates the need for an etic approach to supplement the emic perspective employed by Neusner and Ricks.

The underlying assumption of many scholars is theological: magic is a fraud, while religion "really" exists, as it is a legitimate relationship with God as opposed to one with either paganic or non-existent forces or entities. However, when magic is viewed as a part of religion rather than a separate phenomenon, different conclusions about the story of the plagues emerge. Unlike Neusner and Ricks, P.

---

[29] Ricks, *Ancient Magic and Ritual Power,* p. 143.

Schafer[30] advocates combining a substantive understanding of the term "magic" with a social/functionalist one, and an emic with an etic approach. He is convinced that this combination will prove most fruitful in any attempt to define magic and to understand its relationship to religion. Schafer further asserts that magic is an aspect of religion. These differences in approach lead to a very different conclusion for Schafer concerning the same Exodus account of the plagues. Schafer suggests that the biblical author's point is not that Moses' and Aaron's acts are legitimate and those of the Egyptian magicians are not, but that Moses' and Aaron's performances are more powerful than the magicians' because God is behind them. "Hence, it is not a question of (biblical) religion versus (Egyptian) magic, but of (biblical) magic versus (Egyptian) magic. That the biblical magic is incorporated into the religious system of the Bible does not say that it is not magic. On the contrary, the story shows that despite the clear prohibition [Deut 18:10-11], magic could easily be made presentable, if only it was subordinated to the will and power of God."[31]

Schafer's perspective raises different issues, however. He states that magic had to be combined with theology "in order to enable magic to be integrated into the religious value system of the Bible, in other words, in order to domesticate magic. The inherent ambivalence of theoretically forbidden but actually practiced magic led to this very wise strategy."[32] Thus, according to him, magic in ancient Israel was originally something separate from religion, which was condemned on its own merits, so had to be subsumed into the religious sphere in order ultimately to be acceptable in the biblical world. However, the idea that magic and religion were originally separate seems to contradict his earlier premise that magic is an aspect of religion. Instead, he demonstrates that magic had to *become* an aspect of religion in order to be seen as legitimate, given that the Bible condemns it elsewhere. This begs the questions of why magic was prohibited in the first place; and, if it was, why did it have to be incorporated into the religion at all?

Schafer's more global approach to the study of magic in the Hebrew Bible forms one of the premises of the present work. We aim to improve on his approach in two main areas. First, like the majority of scholars working on the issue, Schafer assumes that magic and religion were originally separate spheres of activity. Current anthropological research, as well as the study of civilizations contemporary with ancient Israel, suggest otherwise. Secondly, Schafer is faced with the task of trying to accommodate the very different perspectives on magic found within the Bible: condemned in some places, clearly practiced (and by biblical heroes) in others.

---

[30] P. Schafer, "Magic and Religion in Ancient Judaism," *Envisioning Magic. A Princeton Seminar and Symposium*, eds. P. Schafer and H. G. Kippenberg (Leiden: Brill, 1997), pp. 19-43.

[31] Schafer, *Envisioning Magic,* p. 29.

[32] Schafer, *Envisioning Magic,* p. 30.

What no scholar of magic in the Bible has considered is that the biblical authors themselves might have differed on the very issues that are so controversial among present-day scholars on the subject of magic. Perhaps the authors did not all view magic in the same way; some might see what we would call "magic" as merely an aspect of religion; others might see certain acts as foreign, and therefore condemn them. In some cases, social context might be all-important.

The present work combines Schafer's method of including emic and etic approaches, substantive and social definitions. However, premises about the relationship between magic and religion are drawn from newer anthropological models of the emergence of both magic and religion in early societies, in addition to studies of magic and religion in ancient Egypt and Mesopotamia. Most previous discussions of magic in the Hebrew Bible have drawn instead on information from later Greco-Roman, New Testament, and Rabbinic societies. Secondly, the present study focuses attention on the implications of source criticism for discussions of magic and religion in the Hebrew Bible. The combination of an understanding of the earliest manifestations of a dichotomy between magic and religion, and an appreciation of the diversity of perspectives represented in the authorship of the Bible, will yield a greater understanding of the nature of magic in the Bible and its relation to Israelite religion.

A Definition of Magic

As we will see, many scholars are reluctant to offer a substantive or qualitative definition of magic. The study of religion by anthropologists and historians is rife with debate over the appropriateness of attempting to delineate a category called "magic" and the validity of the universal applicability of any such definition. However, it is evident from the very fact of their scholarship on the subject that at some level they do have a sense of distinct behaviors, practices, activities, rituals, and objects that can be categorized as "magical." Thus, despite arguments to the contrary, a substantive (as opposed to purely social/functional), etic definition is not only possible, but desirable in order to ensure that we are all describing the same set of phenomena.

The purpose of a definition should be to help identify behavior categorically across time and space, with only minor modifications that take into account emic notions of the concept under discussion. Within the Hebrew Bible, magic can be defined as *an act performed by a person (as opposed to theophany or direct acts of God), with or without attribution to God, that has no apparent physical causal connection to the (expected or actual) result.* These are the types of phenomena that other scholars seem to be describing in their discussions of magic in other fields of study as well as when discussing biblical magic. This definition is etic, substantive, and flexible enough to be universally applicable. At the same time, it does not preclude a discussion of emic or sociological understandings of magic within the

Bible; in fact, the discussion in Chapter Two below will demonstrate its compatibility with emic conceptions of magic in Israel. For example, emic approaches and the application of sociological theories are both essential to understanding the different authorial perspectives on magic; however, it is necessary to identify the behaviors and practices in question substantively before any such investigation can be credibly performed.

Identifying Magic in the Hebrew Bible

Our approach herein attempts to balance a consciousness of the problems inherent in applying modern categories to an ancient world with a scholarly approach to identifying magic in the Hebrew Bible. As we shall see in Chapter One, such categories as "magic," "religion," and "supernatural" simply do not exist in certain places and times; for this reason, many anthropologists have rejected any attempts to classify behavior in this way. In the case of the ancient world, it is difficult to find firm divisions between magical and religious activities until the time of classical Greece, and then those categories refer to social rather than substantive distinctions. The effectiveness of retrojecting later categories onto the worldviews of ancient Israel is questionable, and this problem is pursued in Chapter One.

In Chapter Two we examine the terminology used to denote magical and divinatory activities in the Hebrew Bible. There are specific activities described by words and phrases that recur particularly in the legal materials (Deuteronomy 18 and Leviticus 19-20), where they are prohibited. The questions of what those activities are, and why they are condemned in the Law Codes, motivate much of the chapter. Chapter Three then demonstrates the existence of magic for which no particular terminology is employed; the magic of prophets and "men of God." Biblical figures such as Moses and Elijah are empowered with abilities that defy natural explanation and fall clearly within the boundaries of our definition of magic: they perform feats in which there is no physical causal connection between initiating action and intended result. We look to source criticism to elucidate possible reasons for the tensions between the legal material and the acts of certain prophets.

Chapter Four picks up the theme of source criticism, further exploring the Priestly and Deuteronomic texts. We analyze such priestly rituals as that employed in the case of a suspected *sôṭāh* (Numbers 5) and sacrificial rites of atonement, and discuss the underlying premises on which they operate to determine the magical content of the priestly worldview. The chapter ends with a look at the worldview portrayed by the Deuteronomic History, framed in terms of the Sinai covenant and its attendant blessings and curses, and the causal relationship between sin and exile. Chapter Five outlines our conclusions regarding the place of magic in ancient Israel, and places them in a greater historical context.

By acknowledging differences among the Bible's sources, it is possible to see that there is more than one perspective in ancient Israel with respect to the place of magic. It also becomes apparent that magic is essential to ancient Israel's religious worldview. Adopting the newer anthropological models for understanding the origin of both religion and magic demonstrates that differentiation between the two is a process that occurs over time and is worked out differently, if at all, in every culture. It is crucial to understand, however, that the worldview underlying magical and religious beliefs is essentially the same: there is a supernatural realm that influences ours, to which we can relate, and that acts on us for good or for bad. This is as much a magical worldview as it is a religious one, a fact that becomes apparent when we apply our definition of magic to religious practices at the heart of Israel's religion and culture, their sense of nationhood and their history.

Chapter One

Magic in the Ancient World

Classical Studies, the New Testament, and Rabbinic Judaism

Part of the reason why many scholars maintain a distinction between magic and religion is that this delineation is found within the primary texts that they study. Because accusations of magic in Greece and especially in the Roman Empire were common and prosecutable criminal offences, the problem of differentiating magic from religion in the classical world was an issue with which the ancients themselves had to deal.

In classical Greece, Heraclitus and Plato shared an intense disapproval of magic. Plato greatly anticipated nineteenth century ideas about the difference between magic and religion when he wrote that *goeteia* (sorcery) is characterized by the intention to persuade the gods, when proper religious conduct should leave the gods free choice. However, many Athenian upper class citizens believed strongly in the efficacy of magic and made use of the services of seers and begging priests.[33] Graf points out that in archaic Greece, myths abound with tales of magic potions and spells, with no condemnation attached to them. Yet classical scholars see the root of the dichotomy between (legitimate) religion and (illegitimate) magic in ancient Greece, though of a slightly later period. The term *magos* itself was not introduced until the 6th century BCE and denoted only the foreign religion of the Persians. Graf suggests that it was Greek xenophobia that gave the word negative connotations: "the term *magos* originated not so much from real observation of Persian religion or from the presence of Persian priests on Greek soil, but from the desire to designate certain ritual and ideological attachments as foreign, unwanted, and dangerous, from inside Greek (or Athenian) religion, not from outside it."[34]

Even after the term *magos* was introduced, however, the accuser and the accused did not necessarily agree on whether what was being practiced was "magic" (and therefore forbidden) or "religion." For practitioners of the Greek Magical Papyri, for example, magic was religion.[35] In fact, most classical

---

[33] F. Graf, "Excluding the Charming: The Development of the Greek Concept of Magic," *Ancient Magic and Ritual Power*, eds. M. Meyer and P. Mirecki (Leiden: Brill, 1995, pp. 29-42) pp. 34-35.

[34] Graf, *Ancient Magic and Ritual Power*, p. 36.

[35] A. F. Segal, "Hellenistic Magic: Some Questions of Definition," *Studies in Gnosticism and Hellenistic Religions*, eds. R. Van den Broek and M. J. Vermaseren (Leiden: Brill, 1981, pp. 349-375) p. 373.

scholars argue that a substantive definition for magic in the Greco-Roman world is impossible, as the magical rites and practices were qualitatively no different from pagan ones, and thus it is largely classical scholars who have been calling for definitions of magic that are entirely social and relative in nature. For example, Segal's evaluation of the relationship between magic and religion, and the impossibility of defining magic on a universal or a substantive level, draws exclusively on evidence from the Greco-Roman world, and this leads him to conclude the following: "When magic was viewed as benign it might easily be coterminous with religion, whereas in the crucial contexts where magic was viewed as antagonistic and illegal it was carefully differentiated."[36] Classical scholars point out that accusations of magic more often than not masked social or political motivations for prosecution, rather than any true fear that magic was being practiced.

The issue of accusations of magic, and of whether there is any substance behind the label "magic," is an important one in New Testament scholarship. Jesus and his followers are often depicted as being accused by enemies of practicing magic while supporters deny the charges vehemently. As has been pointed out by several scholars, many of the techniques and feats attributed to Jesus in the Gospels are analogous to well-attested magical practices in the contemporary Greco-Roman world.[37] Not surprisingly, scholars who view Jesus' actions as magical tend to define magic from a more etic (outsider's) standpoint, pointing out the similarities between his various acts of healing and the miracles he performed with behaviors and practices detailed in other ancient texts concerning magicians. Those who defend Jesus against such accusations emphasize the need for an exclusively emic (insider's) approach to appreciate Jesus' actions from the perspective of Jesus himself and those who wrote about him; clearly he was not trying to practice magic but rather acting as the instrument of God to help defeat evil powers.[38] For such scholars, an etic perspective is thus undesirable for the New Testament: "One must avoid identifying phenomena on the basis of external similarities. Instead, one must concentrate on the larger framework of meaning [explicit and implicit] … in which these phenomena appear."[39]

These scholars claim that the question of whether or not Jesus was a magician is irrelevant, because he himself never claimed the title. "The issue is not

---

[36] A. F. Segal, "Hellenistic Magic," p. 359.

[37] See, for example, M. Smith, *Jesus the Magician* (San Francisco: Harper & Row, 1978); and J. M. Hull, *Hellenistic Magic and the Synoptic Tradition* (London: SCM Press, 1974).

[38] H. C. Kee, "Magic and Messiah" in *Religion, Science and Magic In Concert and In Conflict*, eds. J. Neusner, E. S. Frerichs, P. V. McCracken Flesher (New York: Oxford University Press, 1989, pp. 121-141) p. 139.

[39] Kee, *Religion*, "Magic and Messiah," p. 140.

whether the Christians' worldview was magical, but how 'magic' functioned as an experience-ordering symbol within the Christian worldview."[40] The questions we should be asking, such scholars claim, are about how the early Christians themselves understood the difference between magic and miracle, and the answer to this is obviously that the definition of magic must be socially relative (what I do is miracle/religion, what you do is magic) with no actual substance to it. General conclusions that can be drawn about magic in Greece, Rome, and particularly in the New Testament, are therefore that "The charge of magic is likely to be made by legitimate religious leaders against people who are viewed as threatening the social order but who have as yet done no other prosecutable criminal offense."[41]

The question then becomes, beyond social history, what do we actually learn about magic, religion, and the ancient world? Comparative religion does not seem possible without the adoption, to some extent at least, of an etic approach. Certainly an emic understanding of the context of meaning is an important starting point, but works such as M. Smith's *Jesus the Magician* are equally crucial for understanding the universals of the human experience, and the roots of religion in general. For a social historian, certainly the emic perspective is primary. For a historian of religions, however, the etic point of view is indispensable.

One additional area of interest to a discussion of magic in the Hebrew Bible is the study of magic in Rabbinic Judaism. Like magic in the New Testament, this issue is rife with internal contradictions among data derived from a variety of conflicting sources, and results in a reluctance to define magic from anything other than a social point of view. On the one hand, BT *Menaḥot* 65a states that those who sit on the Sanhedrin should be *bāʿaley keŝapim* (masters of magic), and there are tales in the Talmud of rabbis who do practice what looks very much like magic (the creation of a calf, for example; see n. 13). However, there are other places where the practice of magic is specifically condemned.

The Talmud is much more explicit about discussing the boundaries between legitimate and illegitimate magic than other ancient texts. According to J. Seidel, the key difference between what is permitted and what is forbidden seems to be the qualifications of the actor: "Magical action utilizes natural laws in unnatural ways. *Kishuf* implies an abuse of divine/human boundaries; the rabbis felt that only rabbis, and only a select few, could tamper with divine

---

[40] S. R. Garrett, "Light on a Dark Subject and Vice Versa: Magic and Magicians in the New Testament," in *Religion, Science and Magic In Concert and In Conflict*, eds. J. Neusner, E. S. Frerichs, P. V. McCracken Flesher (New York: Oxford University Press, 1989, pp. 142-165), p. 150. Segal writes along similar lines that the issue for scholarship should not be whether charges of magic against Jesus were true, but "to define the social and cultural conditions and presuppositions that allow such charges and counter-charges to be made" (p. 370).

[41] A. F. Segal, "Hellenistic Magic," p. 370.

forces."[42] Neusner concurs: "... the Torah was held to be a source of supernatural power. The rabbis controlled the power of Torah because of their mastery of Torah quite independently of heavenly action. They could issue blessings and curses, create men and animals. They were masters of witchcraft, incantations, and amulets. They could communicate with heaven. Their Torah was sufficiently effective to thwart the action of demons. However they disapproved of magic, they were expected to do the things magicians do."[43]

There is, of course, much disagreement within rabbinic writings about what constitutes legitimate and illegitimate magical practice. In some places, the point of departure seems to be the rabbinic interpretation of Deut 18:10-11, classifying "magic" as the activity of foreigners.[44] Other writings try to be more specific about what is permitted and forbidden, yet the criterion for distinguishing magic from religion still seems to hinge on the status of the practitioner: the "rabbi who is knowledgeable about cosmic semiotics can emulate the deity. Creation *ex nihilo* can be performed by legitimate and legitimized magicians."[45]

Thus, in ancient Greece and Rome, as well as in the New Testament and Rabbinic Judaism, there is a strong case for social/functional definitions of magic as opposed to substantive ones. In all of these societies, "magic" in some sense belonged to the outsiders and developed or maintained a negative connotation for that reason. In Greco-Roman writings it is particularly difficult to find substantive definitions of "magic," and there was no agreement within the culture itself as to what constituted magic, exactly – even the *magi* were understood to be practicing a "religion." The recognition that qualitatively speaking there are essential similarities between what is called "magic" and those activities that fall under the category of permitted religion, is particularly evident in the New Testament and rabbinic sources, both of which are self-conscious about careful delineation of these classifications. In the New Testament, the difference seems

---

[42] J. Seidel, "Charming Criminals: Classification of Magic in the Babylonian Talmud," in *Ancient Magic and Ritual Power*, eds. M. Meyer and P. Mirecki (Leiden: Brill, 1995, pp. 145-166), p. 150.

[43] J. Neusner, "Phenomenon of the Rabbi," *Numen* 16/1 (1969), pp. 1-20. See also M. D. Swartz, *Scholastic Magic: Ritual and Revelation in Early Jewish Mysticism* (Princeton University Press, 1996).

[44] See J. Seidel, "Charming Criminals," p. 148.

[45] J. Seidel, p. 164; he is commenting on the following passage (his translation): "Abaye said, The laws of magicians are similar to those of the Sabbath. Certain activities are punished by stoning, some are not liable to punishment, yet forbidden *a priori*, and others are entirely permitted. Therefore if one actually performs magic he is stoned; if he creates an illusion he is exempt but the action is still forbidden; and what is entirely permitted? Such deeds as were performed by R. Hanina and R. Oshia, who spent every Sabbath evening studying the "Laws of Creation" (*Hilchot Yezira*) by means of which they created a one-third size calf and ate it (BT Sanhedrin 67b)."

to be the alleged source of the power, whether divine or demonic, that determined the legitimacy of the behavior. Over time, and throughout the history of
the Church, this became a matter of "what we do is religion; anything different
is magical and therefore heresy." In Jewish texts, however, the emphasis is on
the status of the practitioner; only very learned and respected rabbis could en-
gage in acts that might be termed "magical," and indeed subject to capital punishment, if practiced by anyone else. Magic elicits fear, as it is devoid of the
moral restrictions inherent to the established (religious) relationship between the
sacred and the profane.

The Hebrew Bible, on the other hand, is not self-reflective in the same way
as the Talmud, New Testament, and classical sources. The prohibitions in Deut
18:10-11 list forbidden activities and practitioners in the context of foreign influences that cannot be tolerated in Israelite religion and society. Yet "magic" of
some sort is clearly practiced by genuine biblical heroes in other stories. For the
biblical authors, there does not seem to be a contradiction here that needs resolv-
ing in the same way that there is for the New Testament authors and the rabbis.
In fact, in the Hebrew Bible the line between magic and religion is much more
blurred, with no single set of criteria to distinguish the two, a fact that is compounded by the different perspectives presented by each biblical author. Most of
the work that has been produced on the subject of magic in the Hebrew Bible
assumes a distinction between magic and religion in ancient Israel analogous to
what classical, New Testament, and Rabbinics scholars find in their sources.
Evidence from civilizations contemporary with biblical Israel, however, suggests
that the dichotomy between magic and religion so prevalent in classical history
was not necessarily apparent in biblical times.

Egypt and Mesopotamia

Evidence from ancient Egypt and Mesopotamia suggests that the dichotomy between magic and religion that is the starting point for many discussions
of magic by contemporary scholars was not necessarily evident in biblical times.
The fact is, in these civilizations that were contemporary with biblical Israel,
magic and religion were only beginning to be differentiated. Evidence especially from Mesopotamia shows that this dichotomy is not an inherent one, but
one that gradually develops over a period of time and is intimately tied to increasing social complexity. In the ancient civilizations of Egypt and Mesopotamia, magic was always part of religion. This is the subject of an important work
by R. Ritner on magic in ancient Egypt,[46] and it is also the implication of some

---

[46] R. K. Ritner, *The Mechanics of Ancient Egyptian Magical Practice*, Studies in Ancient
Oriental Civilization No. 54 (Chicago: The Oriental Institute of the University of Chicago,
1993).

recent scholarship by T. Abusch on the subject of magic and witchcraft in Meso-potamia.[47]

Ritner begins his survey of Egyptian magic with a review of anthropologi-cal and sociological definitions of magic and concludes that none of the current assumptions or terminology apply to ancient Egypt: magic is not stigmatized socially; it is not the property of a fringe group but rather of the entire culture; and it is an essential and inseparable aspect of Egyptian religion. Ritner argues that this does not mean that the category "magic" should be dissolved for Egypt, however, because the Egyptians themselves had a name for it: *heka*. The word *heka* refers to a deity as well as a concept of magic[48] and is attested from Old Kingdom times through the Roman period.

In mythology, Heka is said to be the first of Re-Atum's creations and is the embodiment of the word spoken by Re-Atum to create the cosmos. "Described as a son of the creator, Heka is in actuality the hypostasis of the creator's own power which begets the natural order."[49] The powers of magic can be used by other gods and even by humans to preserve existence and to destroy their ene-mies. The force of *heka* is morally neutral, and even the gods could be threat-ened by it, and they are said to fear it. Magic in this sense is not "supernatural" in that it does not stand apart from the created order: "Productive and destruc-tive, the force of magic animates and permeates the cosmos, resident in the word, in the bodies of gods and men, and in the plants and stones of the earth."[50]

In order to define "magic" for ancient Egypt as a prerequisite for his study of the subject, Ritner examines the terms used by the Egyptians themselves for "magic," "spell," and related concepts. He suggests that the terminology de-notes not just "a thing said" or "a thing possessed," but rather an emphasis on *action*. He concludes: "magic by rite is the logical point of departure for an in-vestigation of the range and significance of Egyptian *hk3*. By focusing upon the magical act rather than the spoken spell, the investigator avoids the subjective

---

[47] T. Abusch, *Babylonian Witchcraft Literature: Case Studies* (Atlanta: Scholars Press, 1987), "Witchcraft and the Anger of the Personal God" in *Mesopotamian Magic: Textual, Historical, and Interpretative Perspectives*, T. Abusch and K. van der Toorn, eds., (Gronin-gen: Styx Publications, 1999), and "The Demonic Image of the Witch in Standard Babylo-nian Literature: The Reworking of Popular Conceptions by Learned Exorcists," in *Religion, Science, and Magic In Concert and in Conflict*, eds. J. Neusner, E. S. Frerichs, P. V. McCracken Flesher (New York: Oxford University Press, 1989), pp. 27-58.

[48] Ritner notes that the use of the term *heka* is inconsistent in that the divine determinative is only occasionally employed to distinguish the god from the concept, and concludes: "So enmeshed are god and concept that little distinction is made between them in Egyptian writ-ings" (pp. 16).

[49] Ritner, *The Mechanics of Ancient Egyptian Magical Practice*, p. 17.

[50] Ritner, *The Mechanics of Ancient Egyptian Magical Practice*, p. 23.

ambiguities [of earlier approaches], and is able to formulate an objective criterion for judging the 'magical' nature of any given act."[51] Thus Ritner's emic
approach (his appreciation of native terminology) provides him with an etic
definition: "for the purpose of this study, any activity which seeks to obtain its
goal by methods outside the simple laws of cause and effect will be considered
'magical' in the *Western* sense."[52]

Ritner recognizes that the need to categorize and classify is a Western one,
and that this study is not one the Egyptians would have been particularly interested in engaging. However, such etic, substantive classification is necessary in
order for us to be able to approach the subject from the perspective of modern
scholarship. At the same time, the emphasis on magic as *activity* is derived from
an emic appreciation of Egyptian magic. In his concluding chapter, Ritner also
notes that the concept of "the simple laws of cause and effect" are Western ones,
and therefore our understanding of magic cannot quite conform to the Egyptian
notion of *heka*: for the Egyptians, *heka* is what underlies *all* causality.

After an extensive and exhaustive survey of Egyptian practices that fall
under his definition of "magic," Ritner concludes that, contrary to earlier definitions of magic, there is no difference in terminology, technique, or efficacy of
private vs. public magic, and that magic and religion intersect and intertwine not
only in practice but also in the person of the practitioner, "for as the priest was
the author and compiler of magical spells and rites, so he was also the performer
and 'magician.'"[53] Although any individual was capable of wielding magic, the
elaborate spells and preparations were recorded in writing, and priests were the
only literate people in ancient Egypt, thereby limiting the practice of magic to
the literate priesthood. The "religious" rites performed by priests in temples
were in many cases identical with the "magical" rituals they performed for individual clients outside the temple walls. Thus, magic was never considered illegitimate in Egypt until the Roman period, when all magic was prohibited, and
particularly under Christianity, when all other religions were seen as heretical.

Similar trends appear in ancient Mesopotamia. There is a great deal of
scholarship detailing Mesopotamian magic in general.[54] Change in Mesopota-

---

[51] Ritner, *The Mechanics of Ancient Egyptian Magical Practice*, p. 69.

[52] Ritner, *The Mechanics of Ancient Egyptian Magical Practice*, p. 69.

[53] Ritner, *The Mechanics of Ancient Egyptian Magical Practice*, p. 220.

[54] See J. A. Scurlock, *Magical Means of Dealing with Ghosts in Ancient Mesopotamia* (Ph.D.
diss., Chicago, 1988); T. Abusch and K. Van der Toorn, *Mesopotamian Magic: Textual,
Historical, and Interpretative Perspectives* (Groningen: Styx Publications, 1999); R. Caplice,
The Akkadian Namburbi Texts: An Introduction, (Malibu, CA, 1974); A. L. Oppenheim, *The
Interpretation of Dreams in the Ancient Near East* (Philadelphia, 1956); E. Reiner, *Šurpu: A
Collection of Sumerian and Akkadian Incantations* (Beiheft 11:Graz, 1958); E. K. Ritter,
"Magical-Expert (= āšipu) and Physician (=asû)," *in Studies in Honor of Benno Landsberger*

mia was much more sweeping than in Egypt, making it difficult to generalize characteristics of magical (or religious) practice over long periods of time. Certain trends have been observed, however, and characterized particularly by T. Abusch.[55] As in Egyptian literature, texts from the Standard Babylonian period (first millennium BCE) demonstrate that the main professional magicians were priests. These "incantation-priests," known as *āšipu*, were exorcists, magicians, and often members of the temple personnel who hired themselves out to private clients. Unlike Egyptian magic, however, non-professionals often employed magic for themselves, without the involvement of *āšipu*. This gave rise to the phenomenon of the *kaššāp(t)u*, the witch, whose magic was usually considered illegitimate and harmful. *Āšipu* were typically employed to undo the evil performed by these witches, although it was acknowledged that the magic techniques themselves were the same for both *āšipu* and *kaššāpu*; the difference was the intention and purpose of the magic, whether harmful or healing. This is an important difference from Ritner's findings in Egypt, and the social conditions giving rise to this difference would form an interesting study themselves. The relevance for the present study is that the perspectives in different parts of the Bible bear similarities to the status of magic in both of these civilizations contemporary with ancient Israel.

Abusch traces the process of polarization of *āšipu* and *kaššāpu* over time, and notes that, both in the cosmic ideology of temple-centered religion and in the imperial urban contexts, two main trends are apparent. First, the powers of both the *āšipu* and the *kaššāpu* increased tremendously, to the point that the magic of the laity was no longer perceived as effective enough to compete or counter either professional practitioner. Secondly, the image of the witch became extremely demonized, as all legitimate magic power - that is, power rightfully granted by the gods - gradually centralized in the hands of the temple-affiliated *āšipu*.

According to Abusch, the witch was originally a practitioner of magic in popular religious conceptions, who was not necessarily understood as evil. "But at some point, perhaps in the early second millennium, witchcraft became a concern of the *āšipu*, perhaps because the female witch had changed her character but more likely because of the expanding role of the male *āšipu* as a result of the increasing centralization and stratification of state, temple, and economy."[56] Abusch compares several editions of a diagnostic *āšipu* text (*BAM* 315) to dem-

---

(Assyriological Studies 16: Chicago, 1965) pp. 299-321; J. Bottéro, "Les Morts et l'au-delà dans les rituels en accadien contre l'action des 'revenants,'" *Zeitschrift für Assyriologie* 73 (1983) pp. 153–203.

[55] See especially "The Demonic Image of the Witch in Standard Babylonian Literature," and "Witchcraft and the Anger of the Personal God."

[56] "Witchcraft and the Anger of the Personal God," p. 84.

onstrate the way in which a composition that originally attributed the anger of personal gods as the primary cause of misfortune was revised and adapted first to include witchcraft in the diagnosis, and then in its latest edition (*SBTU* 2, 22) to present witchcraft as the primary diagnosis and cause.[57] He indicates that the increasing selection of witchcraft as the diagnosis of choice arose as a consequence of the growing importance of the belief in and fear of witchcraft as a purely malevolent strain of magic.

Abusch theorizes that concern with the powerful enmity of other human beings replaces the personification of external threats in the form of demons (found primarily in Sumerian incantation literature), as increasing social complexity leads to the sense that dangers derive from within society rather than solely from nature.[58] Thus witchcraft beliefs, which originated in popular forms of religion, were integrated into the system of *āšipūtu* in which power belongs to and derives from the gods. Thus the witch, being human, became demonized and portrayed as an opponent of the gods. "In *āšipūtu*, the witch's growing power over humans and their personal gods is recognized but is, then overcome by the great gods and their priestly emissaries, to whom individual members of the community can now turn for justice and assistance."[59] Thus, as religion comes under state control with the advent of central temples and official priesthoods, laypeople able to access divine sources of power for their own ends were increasingly understood as malevolent forces and blamed for societal ills. In this way, the power of divine mediation was secured in the hands of professionals such as the *āšipu*.

Scurlock notes the distinct overlap between our categories of "magic" and "religion' when applied to Mesopotamia.[60] Scholars tend to refer to priestly activities such as maintenance of the daily cult and the celebration of festivals as "religious," whereas problem-oriented rituals are termed "magical." "It should be kept in mind, however, that these two types of activity were part of the same belief system and that there was none of the hostility between them to be seen in later times between 'magic' and 'religion.' Exorcists and priests received the

---

[57] Abusch discerns the same development in prayers and incantations, rewritten over time to include witchcraft as a source of misfortune. See his *Babylonian Witchcraft Literature*, pp. 9-46 and 61-74.

[58] "Witchcraft and the Anger of the Personal God," pp. 108 and 111.

[59] "Witchcraft and the Anger of the Personal God," p. 114.

[60] J. Scurlock, *Magical Means of Dealing with Ghosts in Ancient Mesopotamia*.

same education, served the same gods, and regarded each other as legitimate practitioners."[61]

Hittite religion displays the same relationship between magic and religion as Egyptian and Mesopotamian religions. As in Mesopotamia, magic was a divine gift and could legitimately be used to placate angry gods.[62] In Hittite texts, magic and religion "are completely intermingled and it is sometimes difficult to say what is religion and what is magic."[63] Analogous to the situation in Egypt, magic is widespread and completely integrated into the Hittite worldview, but kept under strict control and limited by priests and priestesses. It was considered illegal for others to practice magic, with capital punishment standard for those who tried. As in first millennium Mesopotamia, there was a careful differentiation between black magic (*alwanzatar*) performed by a sorcerer (*alwanzinaš*) and white magic performed by legitimate practitioners, with the former strictly against the law.[64]

As valuable as this comparative information would seem to be for scholars of magic in the Hebrew Bible, evidence from these civilizations contemporary with ancient Israel does not inform most other explorations of this topic. The comparative information of choice is rather derived from classical studies, sometimes drawing from New Testament and rabbinic scholarship as well. However, Egypt and Mesopotamia, cultures that were contemporary with biblical religion, are a much better starting point for understanding magic in ancient Israel than classical studies. By the Greco-Roman period, there was a definite dichotomy between magic and religion that, although assumed for the Hebrew Bible, is not represented in contemporary ancient Near Eastern literatures. The fact that most of the scholars writing on magic in ancient Israel draw from the plethora of studies on Greek and Roman magic to form their conclusions about biblical magic, causes them to read more modern definitions of magic and its distinction from religion into the Hebrew Bible.

---

[61] J. A. Scurlock, "Magic: Ancient Near East," in *The Anchor Bible Dictionary* (New York: Doubleday, 1992).

[62] D. H. Engelhard, *Hittite Magical Practices: An Analysis* (Ph.D. diss: Brandeis, 1970), pp. 105-113.

[63] A. S. Kapelrud, "The Interrelationship between Religion and Magic in Hittite Religion," Numen 6 (Leiden: Brill, 1959) p. 33.

[64] See the Hittite Laws in *ANET* pp. 188-97.

Anthropological Discussions of Magic

Compounding the influence of classical, New Testament, and Rabbinic scholarship on the subject of magic, the widespread presupposition that magic and religion constitute separate realms of behavior in ancient Israel is also traceable to the
influence of early anthropological characterizations of both magic and religion, and
the ethnocentric biases against magic that were inherent in these early definitions of
the term.   Ironically, it is these nineteenth century pioneers of the field that have
made a lasting impression on historians of religion.   Current approaches and perspectives on magic and its relation to religion have had little or no influence on
current magic scholarship in any field of research other than anthropology.   It is
these more modern anthropological perspectives, however, that hold the most
promise for a fruitful investigation of magic in ancient societies.

Early anthropological definitions of magic begin with E. B. Tylor.[65] Tylor
views magic as a "pseudo-science" that postulates a direct cause-effect relationship between magical act and desired event. Tylor is well-known for his application of evolutionary theories to the development of religion and culture; his
scheme involves a gradual progression from primitive to modern thought in the
history of humans, which in religious terms culminates in monotheism (Christianity in particular) and culturally in the modern Western scientific world. This
evolutionary perspective not only views magic as inferior to religion and science
but separates magic from religion as an entirely different type of activity. Tylor's
ideas deeply influenced the ideas of J. G. Frazer, whose *Golden Bough*[66] laid the
groundwork for much of the subsequent research into the relationship between
magic and religion, and the definitions of each of these terms.

Frazer explicitly details the evolutionary nature of the cultural development
of humanity through stages of social, mental and religious development that
begin with magic, progress to religion, and finally culminate in the empirical
understanding of natural laws. He defines magic as a technique of coercion in
which the practitioner's attitude toward the spirit world is a threatening one, in
actions expected to yield automatic results. This is in direct contrast with religion, in which the attitude is pious and propitiatory. The legacy of this dichotomy
and negative characterization of magic is evident in the scholarship of many of
the contemporary historians of religion discussed above. For Frazer, all magical
practices, from any culture or time period, are "pathetic or ludicrous."[67]

---

[65] E. B. Tylor, *Primitive Culture: Researches into the Development of Mythology, Philosophy, Religion, Art and Custom* (London: John Murray, 1873).

[66] J. G. Frazer, *The Golden Bough. Part 1, The Magic Art and the Evolution of Kings* (New
York: the Macmillan Company, 1910).

[67] Frazer, *The Golden Bough*, p. 127.

The legacies of Tylor and Frazer can be observed chiefly among the anthropologists who followed in their wake and are particularly evident in the work of B. Malinowski.[68] Malinowski views the issue from a socio-cultural perspective rather than an evolutionary or historical one but maintains and enforces the dichotomy between magic and religion, retains the derogatory characterization of magical practice, and continues to uphold the validity of his definition as a universal one. According to Malinowski, magic is directly and essentially concerned with the psychological needs of the individual rather than of the community or nature. Magic focuses on specific, concrete problems. Religion deals instead with the fundamental issues of human existence and questions of salvation, death, and the meaning of existence, as opposed to the more immediate goals of magic such as controlling the weather, promoting health, or achieving status. Magic is instrumental in nature, characterized by manipulation and attempts to control nature, while religion is expressive.

Such strict categorization certainly does not hold for Egypt, and would place sacrifice rituals intended to enhance the fertility of the land, for example, or a rain-dance, in the realm of magic. Yet for some peoples, such activities were cyclical events on their religious calendar. Such definitions are too strict, inflexible, and ultimately ethnocentric to accommodate a variety of cross-cultural experiences. They are, however, an improvement over the evolutionary schemes that preceded them.

The work of anthropologist E. E. Evans-Pritchard[69] is a turning point in the history of scholarship on the subject of magic. Like Malinowski, Evans-Pritchard still emphasizes the functional role of magic, but he reacts against the idea that there can be a single, universally-valid definition of magic. Evans-Pritchard also rejects the idea that magic and religion are distinct categories, maintaining that magic is an integral part of both religion and culture. He argues that the dichotomy between the two reflects an ethnocentric distinction between "natural" and "supernatural" which is not made in most religions, and thus the idea that magic is something separate from (and inferior to) religion is largely untenable.

Evans-Pritchard's revolution in the study of magic has had a lasting influence on current scholarship. In addition to advocating the abandonment of the terms "religion" and "magic" altogether,[70] Evans-Pritchard initiated two other

---

[68] B. Malinowski, *Magic, Science and Religion and Other Essays* (New York: Doubleday, 1948), and *A Scientific Theory of Culture and Other Essays* (Chapel Hill: University of North Carolina Press, 1965).

[69] E. E. Evans-Pritchard, *Theories of Primitive Religion* (Oxford: Clarendon Press, 1965); *Witchcraft, Oracles, and Magic among the Azande* (Oxford: Clarendon Press, 1937).

[70] *Theories of Primitive Religion*, p. 111.

approaches to the study of magic. First, he emphasized the social processes that surround accusations of magic, concluding that magic is an important force in sustaining a society by providing an expedient explanation for misfortune. Like the classical scholars heavily influenced by his work, Evans-Pritchard stressed the normative role of magical beliefs in maintaining the moral system and social codes of the Zande he studied. Secondly, Evans-Pritchard was the first to advance an emic approach to cultural study. He advocated an exclusively emic perspective, indicating the relative nature of definitions of terms such as "magic" and "religion," terms which according to him have no universal validity and should be abandoned altogether. The irony is that those who tried to follow in his footsteps have since universally applied his definitions of these terms.

The majority of scholars working on the subject of magic in ancient societies argue along with Evans-Pritchard that the only responsible type of scholarship is to attempt to view the issue from the perspective of those who use the term "magic" and derive a definition from there, one that is strictly relative to the society under study. J. Neusner, for example, advocates this kind of definition when he states that the distinction between magic and religion flows from a system's judgment of who or what are "in," and who or what are "out" (religion being "in," and magic "out")[71], and all scholars who argue that a universal definition is an impossibility are implicitly suggesting that emic definitions are the only valid ones. This approach is particularly emphasized among historians of the Hellenistic world. A. F. Segal, for example, states that "no definition of magic can be universally applicable because 'magic' can not and should not be construed as a properly scientific term. Its meaning changes as the context in which it is used changes. No single definition of magic can be absolute, since all definitions of magic are relative to the culture and sub-culture under discussion."[72]

A corollary to the emic approach, evident particularly in classical scholarship, is the tendency to turn to sociological theories to define magic. Evans-Pritchard's promotion of an emic perspective still allowed him to qualitatively classify certain practices within Zande society as "magical," although his discussion of magic is largely from a social/functional perspective. Others who looked to sociology to help define "magic" soon began to do so exclusively, however, at the expense of more substantive definitions. Rather than looking for substantive markers of behaviors and practices to determine the category

---

[71] J. Neusner, "Science and Magic, Miracle and Magic in Formative Judaism: The System and the Difference," in *Religion, Science and Magic In Concert and in Conflict*, eds. J. Neusner, E. S. Frerichs, P. V. McCracken Flesher (New York: Oxford University Press, 1989), pp. 62-63.

[72] A. F. Segal, "Hellenistic Magic: Some Questions of Definition," *Studies in Gnosticism and Hellenistic Religions*, eds. R. Van den Broek and M. J. Vermaseren (Leiden: Brill, 1981, pp. 349-375), pp. 350-51.

"magic," scholars like E. Durkheim[73], and M. Mauss[74] suggest that the term "magic" is applied within a society to delineate anti-social and illegal behavior. Durkheim and Mauss prefer to distinguish the categories of "sacred" and "profane." For them, "sacred" comprises both religion, defined as a collective system of beliefs and practices, and magic, which they define as privately performed ritual and non-collective beliefs. Thus the distinction between magic and religion for these scholars is a social, rather than a substantive one. Durkheim and Mauss are followed by many historians of religion, beginning with M. Eliade[75], and more recently by J. Z. Smith[76] and others[77] who view magic in antiquity as not marked by any particular attitudes, behaviors, or actions, but rather as a category used exclusively to label deviant and illegitimate beliefs and practices. J. Neusner follows along the same lines when he distinguishes religion from magic by stating that the difference is between "what is normative and what is aberrational in religious situations."[78] Smith goes even further, stating that "illegality is the one universal characteristic of magic,"[79] and argues that because of this, there is "little merit in continuing the use of the substantive term 'magic' in second-order, theoretical academic discourse."[80]

Since the time of Evans-Pritchard there has been a backlash against the nineteenth century ethnocentrism that saw magic as a category compatible with a universal definition and worthy only of scorn. Evans-Pritchard's emphasis on an exclusively emic approach has found widespread acceptance among many

---

[73] E. Durkheim, *The Elementary Forms of the Religious Life* (New York: The Macmillan Co., 1965; reprint of 1915).

[74] M. Mauss, *A General Theory of Magic*, translated by Robert Brain (London: Routledge and Kegan Paul, 1972).

[75] M. Eliade, *The Sacred and the Profane* (New York: 1959).

[76] J. Z. Smith, "Good News is no News," in *Map is Not Territory. Studies in the History of Religions*, ed. J. Z. Smith (Leiden: Brill, 1978) pp. 190-207.

[77] For example D. E. Aune, "Magic in Early Christianity," *ANRW* II. 23.2 (1980) pp. 1507-1557, defines magic as "that form of religious deviance whereby individual or social goals are sought by means alternate to those normally sanctioned by the dominant religious institution."

[78] J. Neusner, "Introduction" in *Religion, Science and Magic in Concert and in Conflict*, p. 5.

[79] J. Z. Smith, *Map is not Territory*, p. 192. Note that this definition of magic not only ignores evidence about magic from ancient Egypt and Mesopotamia, but also excludes many legendary magicians from being classified as such, including the Egyptian magicians from Exodus 7-9 as well as Merlin, Glenda the Good Witch, and Cinderella's fairy godmother.

[80] J. Z. Smith "Trading Places," in *Ancient Magic and Ritual Power*, eds. M. Meyer and P. Mirecki (Leiden: Brill, 1995, pp. 13-27), p. 16.

modern scholars. For Evans-Pritchard, "magic" can only be evaluated and classified within a given society, but for him there are, within each society, qualitative markers of what constitutes magic. Many modern scholars combine Evans-Pritchard's emphasis on an emic approach with sociological theories of deviance, eclipsing any substantive definitions of magic in favor of purely social/functional ones. Evans-Pritchard's suggestion that the category "magic" should be dissolved has been taken in two different ways by subsequent scholars as well. Like Smith, scholars who combine the emic perspective with Durkheim's sociological approach claim that the term is no longer useful because "magic" resists a universal and substantive definition: even within a given culture, the only behavior that the term "magic" signifies is whatever is aberrational, illegal, and generally frowned upon by the dominant religious group.

As different as the theories of Smith, Neusner, and other modern scholars are from those of nineteenth century scholarship on the subject of magic, they share in common the assumption that magic and religion are distinct phenomena. Other anthropologists and historians have taken issue with this dichotomy and the evolutionary perspective that originated it, and it is their work that informs the current study, and is in turn informed by new anthropological theories of the origins of magic.

One anthropologist in particular has been critical of past efforts to understand the relationship between magic and religion, including Israelite religion. M. Douglas has written prolifically on the subject of magic and argues strongly against evolutionary schemes that relegate magic to more primitive levels of culture, and religion to more advanced societies.[81] Douglas blames Frazer and Malinowski for insisting that magic and religion were irreconcilably opposed; she accuses Frazer of sending the discipline of comparative religion "into a blind alley" with his mistaken definition of magic as automatic efficacy.[82] In her analysis of Israelite religion, she notes that Priestly theology is replete with magical ritual aimed at dealing with impurity,[83] and that the principle of divine

---

[81] See M. Douglas, *Purity and Danger* (London: Routledge and Kegan Paul, 1966; reprinted 1979); "Deciphering a Meal" in her *Implicit Meanings: Essays in Anthropology* (London: Routledge and Kegan Paul, 1975) pp. 249-275; and *Natural Symbols: Explorations in Cosmology* (New York: Pantheon Books, 1982 [reprint of 1970]).

[82] *Purity and Danger*, pp. 19, 58-59. Douglas is equally critical of W. Robertson Smith, who (influenced by Tylor and Frazer) relegated such "irrational" (from a Protestant standpoint) ideas as rules of impurity to early stages of primitive thought, since provisions to deal with uncleanness were magical in nature. Magical ritual, expected to have automatic effect, was irrational and meaningless (see *Purity and Danger*, pp. 17-18) in a nineteenth-century perspective convinced that in the evolutionary development of religion, Christianity peaked when it progressed beyond Catholicism to Protestantism.

[83] *Purity and Danger*, pp. 25-26, and especially Chapter Three, "The Abominations of Leviticus" (pp. 41-57).

retribution at the heart of the Deuteronomistic History itself presupposes the "efficacious" nature of human actions.[84] Thus the Frazerian dichotomy scholars perceive between magical efficacious action and religious ethical will is a false one; in the Hebrew Bible, religion and magic overlap as elements of a symbolic system of social communication that defies compartmentalization. Ritual enactment occurs in both sacred and profane social institutions and is in fact the basis of all social communication.[85]

Several historians of religion have been similarly critical of Frazer's influence in their discipline. For example, O. Pettersson demonstrates that any attempt to show an evolutionary pattern from magic to religion is misguided and depends entirely on norms dictated by 19th-20th century Christianity.[86] He states that "the ideas behind 'magical' rites and beliefs are the same as those lying behind 'religious' beliefs and practices." D. Hammond takes this further, defining magic as simply one element of religion, an aspect that expresses belief in human powers as effective forces alongside the powers of spiritual beings, and the dynamic forces of the physical universe.[87] In a recent symposium on the subject of magic, the editors of the resulting anthology described a "growing consensus among the participants that magic cannot, and should not, be distinguished from religion as a separate force, that it has always been regarded as part of the religious sphere, no matter whether one looks at it approvingly or disapprovingly."[88]

In an important article, H. S. Versnel reviews the state of the field and proposes a solution to the current lack of consensus about approaches to the study of magic, and the need for a definition.[89] His conclusions underlie much of the approach herein to identifying magic. Versnel questions the practicality of employing social function as a method of categorization for the reason that "practically no scholar using the functionalist approach manages to elaborate his social interpretation of magic without using the term 'magic' in one or the other of the

---

[84] Douglas, *Purity and Danger*, p. 50. Douglas' suggestions inspire and underlie much of our discussion of Priestly magic in Chapter Four.

[85] Douglas, *Purity and Danger*, p. 72ff.

[86] O. Pettersson, "Magic – Religion; Some marginal notes to an old problem" *Ethnos* 22, 1957, pp. 109-119.

[87] D. Hammond, "Magic: A Problem in Semantics," *American Anthropologist* 72, 1970, pp. 1349-56.

[88] P. Schafer and H. G. Kippenberg, *Envisioning Magic. A Princeton Seminar and Symposium* (Leiden: Brill, 1997) p. xi.

[89] H. S. Versnel, "Some Reflections on the Relationship Magic-Religion," *Numen* 38, Dec. 1991, pp. 177-197.

more conventional substantive meanings."[90]   He does acknowledge the usefulness of a sociological approach, particularly for some societies, but argues that this does not preclude the existence of other more substantive implications of the term "magic." He also suggests a combination of emic and etic approaches; one should try to understand magic from the perspective of the culture under study, yet be aware that in order to express observations and conclusions one must use one's own points of reference. And lastly, he states that the categories "magic" and "religion" often blur, but it is not practical to avoid using the term "magic" altogether. Versnel concludes that the only realistic alternative is to produce a working definition of the concept, recognizing that any definition needs continuous readjustment as new data come to light.

Versnel suggests the employment of a broad category with a long list of ideal traits, "a polythetic classification."[91]   When enough of these traits are present in the behavior being studied, one can employ the category, for "Just like religions, 'magical' practices or expressions may share some though not all family resemblances. This means that we may accept a 'broad, polythetic or prototypical' definition of magic, based on a 'common sense' collection of features."[92]

Versnel does not offer his own definition but, applying his own suggestions to a brief examination of magic and religion in ancient Greece, uses the general characteristics attributed to magical behavior by the Greeks themselves. The Greeks had what we would (and scholars do) call "magic" ("manipulations, charms, gestures, application of secret texts, compulsory action through the use of secret names of gods or demons, etc. etc."[93]), and no one questions the existence of a Greek "religion." Although the Greeks employed both categories the lines are very often blurred between the two, as the same activity could be labeled "magic" by one group and "religion" by another; hence the usefulness of sociological definitions of magic. However, as we saw in our discussion of magic in classical societies, Versnel points out that the Greeks had specific ideas of what qualitatively differentiated one from the other, even if they rarely all agreed. Thus dissolving the category "magic" altogether is not useful; it is more interesting to note when the differences are discernable, as well as when the

---

[90] Versnel, "Some Reflections," p. 187.

[91] Versnel refers to L. Wittgenstein's formulation of this type of classification system in *Philosophical Investigations* (New York 1958, translated from the German ed. 1953), pp. 66-67. He also points out that W. P. Alston makes good use of this type of categorization in his discussion of "Religion" in *Encyclopedia of Philosophy*, vol. 7 (1967) p. 142, as does J. Z. Smith in "Fences and Neighbors: Some Contours of Early Judaism," in his *Imagining Religion: From Babylon to Jonestown* (Chicago, 1982) pp. 1-18.

[92] Versnel, "Some Reflections," p. 186.

[93] Versnel, "Some Reflections," p. 189.

lines blur between "magic" and "religion," and to ask why. The social/functional assessment in the differentiation between magic and religion is important but by no means entails the necessity of rejecting the concept of magic for use in comparative research, for the simple reason that charges of magic (both in antiquity, as well as in the modern world) always refer to substance.[94]

Versnel's summary and conclusions about the current state of magic research are incorporated in the present work. Still lacking in all discussions of magic in the ancient world, and integral to the present study, is current anthropological research on the origins of magic and religion. As evidenced by our earlier discussions, the anthropological point of departure for any historical study of magic and religion still seems to be a combination of the approaches of Tylor, Frazer, Malinowski and Evans-Pritchard. Ironically, many contemporary anthropologists have developed entirely different perspectives on magic and religion that are much more relevant to studies of ancient religion, and in fact share much in common with the conclusions about Egyptian and Mesopotamian religion and magic of Ritner and Abusch.

Within the last fifty years, anthropological discussions of religion have largely centered on the topic of shamanism. The term shamanism is applied not only to the religious activities of today's "primitive" societies. The worldviews and practices subsumed under this category have also been retrojected to ancient societies with similar artifacts and, where documented, analogous belief systems. In fact, when archaeologists and paleoanthropologists describe the beliefs and practices that seem to have given rise to the earliest art, including cave paintings and stone carvings, they use the terms "shamanic" or "shamanistic" far more often that "magical" or "religious." The view is that shamanism is the origin of both magic and religion.[95] The shaman is an inspired religious leader, and his position as magician, healer, and priest only branched into these specialties as society became increasingly complex.[96]

The suggestion that magic and religion share a common origin nullifies much of the current debate over the definitions of each and boundaries between

---

[94] Versnel, "Some Reflections," p. 190.

[95] La Barre, *The Ghost Dance*, p. 161.

[96] A good discussion of the evolution of priesthood is found in T. W. Driver, *The Magic of Ritual: Our Need for Liberating Rites that Transform our Lives and Our Communities* (New York, HarperCollins, 1991) pp. 69-71. Driver demonstrates that the origin of "priestly types" such as "the preacher, pastor, rabbi," or "imam" are adaptations of the shaman to "hierarchical patterns of social organization. We should associate the priestly type with the rise of kingship, the priest being a shaman who has become "courtly" finding a place within the ranks of the king's ministers ... shamanism [in these societies] is left to 'outsiders.'"

the two. It also changes the course of an investigation into their relationship from one of finding similarities and differences, to one that instead pursues the questions of when and why the two bifurcated within a given society. Or, in the case of ancient Egypt, why they never really did.

As we discussed in the Introduction, the difference between magic and religion, outside of the social forces that act on both and seek to separate the two, is largely a matter of who controls supernatural events. Within the boundaries of "religion," supernatural phenomena are attributed directly to gods or spirits, while practitioners of "magic" are attributed with the ability to manipulate those forces. Magic and religion, therefore, can and do coexist within a given society. For some cultures, there is no distinction between the effects brought about by specially trained or gifted humans and those caused by gods or spirits. Ancient Egypt offers an excellent example of this; the term *heka* itself applies equally to the power wielded by priests, manifested by gods, and inherent in the natural world. Other cultures impose a dichotomy between "magic" and "religion," but draw the line at different points depending on such variables as the nature of the practitioner, the type of act, and the source of power. This is exemplified in ancient Mesopotamia where priests and witches employed the same techniques, yet the *āšipu* were professionals associated with a religious temple, while the *kaššāpu* were illegitimate practitioners, and their magic considered harmful.

The essential problem in delineating the differences between magic and religion - whether from etic, emic, or social/functional perspectives - is that it is difficult to pin down distinctions that apply readily across cultures and history. Versnel's suggestion of a polythetic classification is one possible solution. But if we look at the essence of both magic and religion, we can discern a common origin that shifts the discussion from one of ideal traits to an evolutionary perspective on the origin of their bifurcation. Both magic and religion are rooted in a relationship between the profane and the sacred that consists of individuals in the profane who acquire or manipulate powers of the sacred in order to cause desired effects in ordinary reality.

Now if we go back to the origins of our species and the first indication that we had a belief in an ultimate (sacred) reality, then we observe no distinction between magic and religion. The cave art of our remotest ancestors marks the beginning of our relationship with the sacred, one in which the distinction between magic and religion is a non-issue. The individuals who are the mediators between the sacred and the profane are the shamans, and this function is one that is ubiquitous throughout time and space in "primitive" societies. Thus the shaman in his or her capacity as mediator between the sacred and the profane performs healings, magical rituals, and sacred rites. It is only with the evolution of more complex societies that the distinction between magic and religion as well as the division of the shaman's functions into various sub-specialties (healers, priests, seers, necromancers, sorcerers, etc.) arises. At this point, religion adopts the social function of maintaining the hierarchy and morality within a society according to the dictates of sacred (spiritual) characters. With religion, the sacred imposes its view on the profane and legitimizes the structure of society.

The individuals now in charge of monitoring this sacred order are deemed priests. Socially, "magic" as a separate, negative category is relegated to interactions between the sacred and the profane not sanctioned or endorsed by the religious order, a state of affairs evident in ancient Greece. Magic becomes socially defined as existing outside the realm of the order proscribed by religion. This is why in the Talmud, for example, rabbis can perform magic; they are operating within the religious structure. But non-rabbis who perform the same feats are subject to the harshest punishments. Additionally, as opposed to religion which is morally "good" by its very nature, magic becomes classified as either "black" or "white," good or bad, depending entirely on the nature of its effect and the status of its agent.

Within ancient Israel, the process of separation into religion and magic, priest and magician, is ongoing and different stages of this are represented by the different authors' portrayals of and statements about the practice of magic. The questions to be pursued in the ensuing investigation are, therefore: is the definition of magic offered at the beginning of this chapter a valid one for ancient Israel? Where do the authors of the Hebrew Bible draw the line between "magic" and "religion"? Is there a consensus among the biblical sources about what constitutes magic? Is the practice of magic universally condemned, or do the authors differ on this important point; and if so, why?

Chapter Two

What's the Magic Word?
Biblical Terms Relating to Magic and Divination

What is "magic" according to the Hebrew Bible?

A common approach to the issue of magic in the Hebrew Bible is to state that part of the uniqueness of Israelite religion lies in its prohibition of magic.[97] Defenders of this position argue that while the belief systems of Israel's neighbors are rife with such superstitions, Israel itself strongly condemned mantic practices of any kind, producing a religion free from the concept of manipulation and coercion of the divine realm. In support of this perspective, two important texts serve as evidence: Deuteronomy 18, part of the Deuteronomic Law Code, and Leviticus 19-20, part of the Holiness Code.

In this chapter we will examine both of these legal texts, first to determine what specifically is prohibited. If these texts prohibit magic, determining what particular practices are banned will help us understand how the legal codes define magic. In fact, we will see that both Deuteronomy 18 and Leviticus 19-20 are far more concerned with prohibiting access to supernatural sources of information - i.e., *divination* - than to the practical application of supernatural powers to defy physical laws of cause and effect that we would label magic.

Unlike those who view the legal materials as the Hebrew Bible's last word on the subject of magic, however, we will then turn to the greater context of the Hebrew Bible to investigate the question of why such practices are so strongly condemned in Deuteronomy and Leviticus. We will examine other narratives in which magic and divination prohibited in Israel are successfully practiced both within its borders and by its neighbors.

The Israelites had a surprisingly rich vocabulary to denote a variety of magical practices and practitioners among their neighbors and themselves. In the Bible, the majority of these terms appear in legal contexts. Unfortunately, the authors seem to have presumed that the audience was aware of the activities denoted by each term and do not describe them, merely listing the names of the practices that are prohibited for Israelites. This would not be a problem if in other biblical texts such vocabulary appeared in narratives about the magical powers and beliefs associated with these terms; however, much of this vocabu-

---

[97] Cf., for example: G. von Rad, *Old Testament Theology*, vol. 1, trans. D. M. G. Stalker (Edinburgh/ London: Oliver and Boyd, 1962); Y. Kaufmann, *Toledot ha'emunah hayisra'elit* (Tel Aviv: Bialik Institute-Dvir), Vols. 1-7 (1937-1948). Translated and abridged from the Hebrew by M. Greenberg as *The Religion of Israel* (Chicago: University of Chicago Press, 1960).

lary is not in use outside of legal biblical materials, or exists only in passing references in condemnatory prophetic texts. Thus the scholar is often left with only guesswork based on etymology and context to determine the meaning of the technical vocabulary used in association with magical practices and practitioners in ancient Israel.

With only four exceptions,[98] there is no connection between the major magical events described in the Bible and the Bible's extensive vocabulary for describing such activities. Out of all of the stories of supernatural events - those that Moses and Aaron bring about with their rods, or that Elijah orchestrates, Elisha's feats – none of these magical activities or practitioners bears the labels that are used for magic and magicians elsewhere in the text. This is not as surprising if we consider that most of the terms are found in lists of prohibited activities; it would pose quite a problem if practices that were specifically banned in one text were named in another text as the activities of some of the primary biblical figures. Where we do find stories involving some of the categories of magicians and/or diviners listed in Leviticus and Deuteronomy in narrative contexts, an interesting pattern emerges: the actions of Israelite and non-Israelite magicians and diviners prove effective and viable means of accessing the supernatural for power or information. It is *because* they work that legal and priestly codes prohibit these activities. But, as we will see, prohibiting these activities is not the same thing as not believing in magic; and not even the same as banning magic and divination altogether. The activities listed in the Holiness Code and in the Law Code in fact only restrict access to the divine to qualified personnel: priests and prophets.

Legal Materials

Deuteronomy 18 contains the most comprehensive list of magical terminology of any single passage in the Bible. For this reason, scholarly discussions of magic in the Bible have tended to focus on this list and generalize from it about magic in ancient Israel. This approach is problematic for two reasons. First, although these terms would have had meaning for their intended audience, it is very difficult for us to translate them with any certainty because the practices and practitioners to whom they refer are simply not described in the Bible.[99] For this reason, scholars must resort to word studies and etymology to try to determine the meanings of the terms, which amounts largely to educated guesswork. The problems are then compounded as conclusions based on this guesswork are drawn about the kinds of practices described.

---

[98] Numbers 22; 1 Samuel 6, 28; Ezekiel 21. See below.

[99] There is one exception: in 1 Sam 28 we have a detailed description of the actions of a certain woman of Endor who has *'ôb wĕyiddĕ'ōnî*. See below.

Second, focusing on the prohibitions in Deuteronomy 18, or on any cata-logue of magic practitioners in legal literature, places too much emphasis on the legal material and specialized terminology in the Bible. Viewing the Deuter-onomic Law Code in isolation from other biblical texts, it is easy to conclude that magic and divination are foreign to Israel. Yet the Bible is replete with sto-ries of legitimate divination and magical activities. Moses and Elijah perform amazing magical feats. Joseph's rise to power in Egypt is occasioned by his divinatory activities as a dream interpreter. David repeatedly resorts to divina-tion to determine Yahweh's will. In short, almost every major biblical hero makes use of magic or divination.

The specific terminology in the Law Code's list of prohibited activities is not found in these stories, however. Deuteronomy 18 provides a detailed list of practices which it identifies as foreign and therefore not to be employed in Is-rael. The only other list of magical activities in legal materials is contained in the Holiness Code (Leviticus 19-20) and a comparison of the terms, contexts, and ultimate purposes of the prohibitions in each is instructive.

In Deuteronomy 18, the list of prohibited activities begins in v. 10, interest-ingly with an activity not usually associated by scholars with magic: the passing of a child through fire (*maʿăbîr běnô ŭbittô bāʾēš*). The meaning of this phrase has long been a question for scholars, and there are a variety of possible an-swers. The first and perhaps most widely accepted possibility is that this is a reference to child sacrifice.[100] The difficulty with this understanding is that the rest of this chapter deals with supernatural actions and/or means of obtaining information.[101] Another possible interpretation of this activity is as a kind of oracle ordeal with divinatory power.[102] This first item on the list demonstrates

---

[100] So G. von Rad, *Deuteronomy*, trans. D. Barton (Philadelphia: Westminster Press, 1973); P. C. Craigie *The Book of Deuteronomy* (Grand Rapids, Michigan: Eerdmans, 1976); A. D. H. Mayes *Deuteronomy* (Grand Rapids, Michigan: Eerdmans, 1979); and W. L. Holladay, *A Concise Hebrew and Aramaic Lexicon of the Old Testament* (Grand Rapids, Michigan: Eerdmans, 1971).

[101] J. Kuemmerlin-McLean ("Divination and Magic in the Religion of Ancient Israel: A Study in Perspectives and Methodology," [Ph.D. Diss: Vanderbilt University, 1986]) points this out and suggests that "some sort of 'sign' or 'knowledge' was thought to come through the sacrifice." She concludes, however, that "there is no support for this understanding in any of the texts" (p. 65).

[102] J. Kuemmerlin-McLean favors this interpretation, admitting however that the only textual support for it is its placement in the context of other divination techniques. Other supporters for this minority view are S. R. Driver, *A Critical and Exegetical Commentary on Deuteron-omy*, 3rd edition (Edinburgh: T and T Clark, 1895); and M. Weinfeld, "The Worship of Molech and of the Queen of Heaven and its Background" *UF* 4 (1972): 133-58. Weinfeld ("Burning Babies in Ancient Israel," *UF* 10, [1978], pp. 411-13) adds that the vocabulary employed in connection with this phrase elsewhere is not sacrificial.

the difficulty of understanding both the practices to which the terms refer and the possible reasons for their inclusion in this particular list of prohibitions. It is ultimately unclear what, if any, relation this phrase has to magical practice.[103]

The next prohibited activity is more obviously magical: *qōsēm qěsāmîm.* The root *qsm* appears in a variety of biblical contexts[104] and seems to be a general term applied to different magical and divinatory practices.[105] What is interesting is that, in some contexts in which the word is found, it bears no negative connotation. For example, in Prov 16:10 the word *qesem* parallels *mîšpāṭ* and thus might indicate the royal use of lots to obtain a legal decision.[106] Likewise, Jeffers points out that the use of the word in Mic 3:6 should not be seen as derogatory: "the verb in this context most likely means 'to do as a prophet does' without specific reference to the use of any technical means."[107] In v. 11, the charge is laid against those who sell their oracles for profit, not against those who provide oracles through *qesem.*[108] The *Qōsēm* is opposed in 1 Sam 15:23 and 2 Kings 17:17. But, while augury is officially condemned, in the story of Balaam in Numbers 22-24 Balaam's powers of divination are respected.[109]

Deuteronomy 18 casts magicians and diviners in a negative light and attributes such practices in Israel to foreign influence. In fact, *qsm* specialists are elsewhere associated with Philistines (1 Sam 14:19) and Ammonites (Ezek 21:34). They are also attested in Judah, however: the *qōsěmîm* of Judah had divinatory dreams (Jer 29:8), divined answers from God (Mic 3:7), and experienced visions (Zech 10:2). The term *bt qsm* is also found in Aramaic inscriptions, and the practice of *qsm* is mentioned in the context of the *marzēaḥ* at Pal-

---

[103] It is entirely possible that there simply is no connection. Perhaps the Law Code purposely begins this list of forbidden practices with an activity that many Israelites already found abhorrent in order to cast the more widely accepted practices that follow in a negative light.

[104] See, for example, Deut 4:16-18; Isa 3:2; 44:25; Mic 3:7, 11; Jer. 14:14; 27:9; 29:8.

[105] BDB (890) and KBL (844) translate the noun *qsm* as "divination," and LXX has the general terms *manteoumenos manteian*, suggesting that the phrase should be understood to indicate the overall category of those who practice divination. A. Jeffers (*Magic and Divination in Ancient Palestine and Syria*, Brill: Leiden, 1996) suggests that it originally indicated divination by casting lots (pp. 96-98).

[106] Jeffers, *Magic and Divination in Ancient Palestine and Syria*, p. 96.

[107] Jeffers, *Magic and Divination in Ancient Palestine and Syria*, p. 97, following D. R. Hillers, *Micah* (Philadelphia: Fortress Press, 1984), p. 46.

[108] Jeffers makes this case strongly, and Seidel ("Studies in Ancient Jewish Magic," [Ph.D. Diss.: UC Berkeley, 1996]) concurs, stating that the practice "was apparently part of the official pre-Exilic religion" (p. 23).

[109] See especially Num 22:7-21; Seidel, p. 24, and see below.

myra.[110] Unfortunately, this wide attestation of the term and presumably the practice outside of Israel could be used to confirm its foreignness to ancient Israel, or equally its ubiquity to the entire ancient Near East, including Israel. Seidel argues the former case: "Looking at all this evidence, it seems that the *Qōsēm* and the activities of this type of diviner were not foreign to Israel at all in the pre-exilic period. Diviners such as Balaam may have operated across boundaries, and if Balaam were from the Transjordan or Mesopotamia as several scholars believe ... *Qōsēm* would have truly been 'marginal' to Israel."[111] The use of *qsm* in Israel, according to a variety of narrative and prophetic texts in the Hebrew Bible, indicates it was a familiar practice in Israel.[112] Its condemnation in Deuteronomy 18, along with other magical specialists, also attests to Israel's unofficial recognition of this type of practitioner, presumably a category of diviner. The real question then is not its place of origin, but why legal and some prophetic materials condemn *qsm*. This is the question to which we will return after examining all of the other terms for magical practices that Deuteronomy prohibits in Israel.

The following term is more difficult to interpret because the root is unclear. A *mĕʿônēn* could have something to do with the word "eye," but would it refer to the "evil eye," hypnotism,[113] or divination by observation of natural phenomena?[114] It is also possible to regard *mĕʿônēn* as a denominative from *ʿānān*, "cloud,"[115] which could suggest either one who obtains oracles by observing patterns in clouds, or one who causes clouds and storms to appear.[116] Some translations offer the words "soothsayer,"[117] "enchanter," or, most commonly, "diviner."[118] To compound the problem, an examination of this term in other

---

[110] See Seidel, "Studies in Ancient Jewish Magic," p. 25.

[111] Seidel, "Studies in Ancient Jewish Magic," p. 25.

[112] See, for example, Isa 3:2, where the prophet lists the *qōsēm* along with the warrior, judge, prophet, and old man as important figures in Judah.

[113] Seidel, "Studies in Ancient Jewish Magic," p.27.

[114] For a good summary of possible etymologies and translations, see T. W. Davies, *Magic, Divination and Demonology Among the Hebrews and Their Neighbors*, 1898 (reprint ed., New York: KTAV, 1969), pp. 79-81.

[115] A. Jeffers, *Magic and Divination in Ancient Palestine and Syria* (Brill: Leiden, 1996), p. 78.

[116] Davies, 1898.

[117] RSV, NEB, JPS. Robertson Smith suggests "hoarsely humming soothsayers," based on a possible derivation from an Arabic root for "hoarse sound." See his "On the Forms of Divination and Magic Enumerated in Deut 18:10-11," *Journal of Philology* 14 (1885), p. 119.

[118] LXX has "one who looks for omens," presumably a diviner.

contexts reveals a negative connotation in Jer 27:9, and a strikingly neutral one in Judg 9:37. In general, from all of its uses in the Hebrew Bible[119] the most we can conclude about this word is that it indicates a diviner.

The term *měnaḥēš* presents similar difficulties for the translator, because it can be derived from two different roots: *nḥš* and *lḥš*. Both roots are found separately in other places in the Hebrew Bible, and both are connected with magic and divination.[120] The verb *niḥēš* occurs only in the *piel* and is rendered "to divine" or "to look for omens" in BDB (638) and KBL (610) respectively, and contexts in which the word is found throughout the Bible support this translation.[121] Some scholars suggest that the verb is denominative from *nāḥāš*, "snake," and translate "to divine by snake charming."[122] Seidel points out that the root *nḥš* is attested in inscriptions from Hatra and Palmyra "where it has mantic connotations," and in Ugaritic *mnḥš* is the designation of a professional capable of preventing snake-bites.[123] Thus, like the word *qsm*, the particular meaning of *měnaḥēš* in the Bible is difficult to state with any certainty beyond understanding it as a category of magical or divinatory specialist.

Měkaššēp, the next term for a forbidden practitioner in Deut 18:10, is a Hebrew cognate to Akkadian *kišpū/ kaššāpu*, "sorcerer" or "magician."[124] Although the etymology here is much more certain, the contexts in which the word is found in the Bible do not detail the particular tasks or techniques of the *měkaššēp*. In Exod 7:11 and Dan 2:2, the term is used of foreign magicians and wise men in Egyptian and Babylonian royal courts without any directly negative connotation, except that their powers are ineffective in relation to the power of Yahweh. In other places, for example Deut 18:10; 2 Kings 9:22 / 2 Chron 33:6; and Isa 47:9, 12, *měkaššěpîm* are condemned. Further support for a general view of *kšp* referring to sorcery or "black" magic can be found in an Ugaritic incantation text from Ras Ibn Hani, the goal of which is to cast out a demon pos-

---

[119] In addition to Deut 18:11, 14, the word is found in Lev 19:26; Judg 9:37; 2 Kings 21:6; 2 Chron 33:6; Isa 2:6; Isa 57:3; Jer 27:9; Mic 5:11.

[120] Davies (*Magic, Divination and Demonology*, p. 51) suggests that the root *lḥš* is used in connection with magic, and *nḥš* with divination.

[121] Gen 44:5, 15; 30:27; 1 Kings 20:33; Num 24:1, 23:23 (in which the word *nāḥāš* is parallel to *qesem*). See also Isa 3:3, 20; 26:16; Jer 8:17; Eccl 10:11.

[122] J. McKay, *Religion in Judah Under the Assyrians* (London: SCM Press Ltd., 1973), p. 118.

[123] Seidel, "Studies in Ancient Jewish Magic," p. 29

[124] CAD, vol. 8, 292; 454. Although most scholars see the term as referring to magicians or sorcerers in general, some note the connection in LXX of Deut 18:10 (*pharmakos epaiedon epaoiden*), as well as in Mic 5:11, with herbs or drugs: see Robertson Smith (1884) p. 126, and Driver (1895) p. 225, and more recently, Jeffers (1996) pp. 65-70.

sessing a young man. In it, *kšpm* are addressed as a potential source for the demonic possession.[125]

In the case of Israel, some scholars contend that this term refers mainly to women who practiced "the more sinister forms of magic"[126] on the basis of Exod 22:17(18), in which only the female *mĕkaššēpāh* is mentioned as deserving capital punishment.[127] This is the only place in which female practitioners of magic are singled out, and in fact LXX has *pharmakous*, "sorcerers," implying both genders. Interpreters have historically seized on this as proof of the particularly malevolent nature of magic in the hands of women, and this verse has been cited in support of much oppression and persecution of supposed "witches" and women seen as dangerous in European and early American history. Perhaps the original text implicated both sexes (as does LXX): *mkšp 'w mkšph l' tḥyh*, with haplography in the Hebrew responsible for the singling out of female sorcerers. The ease with which haplography could occur in writing *mkšp 'w mkšph* makes it difficult to conclude that this passage or this term has any special connection to women.[128]

The terms in Deut 18:11 seem to be more specific than those in the previous verse. The first is *ḥōbēr ḥāber*, which most translators relate to the use of charms and spells. It is associated with Babylon in Isa 47:9, 12; and the Akkadian cognate *ubburu* means "to bind magically."[129] This is the more popular derivation of the root among scholars,[130] who relate the term to the known prac-

---

[125] See J. C. de Moor, *An Anthology of Religious Texts from Ugarit* (Leiden: Brill, 1987), pp. 429-432.

[126] J. B. Segal, "Popular Religion in Ancient Israel," *Journal of Jewish Studies* 27 (1976) p. 6.

[127] In addition to Segal, see J. Burden, "Magic and Divination in the Old Testament and their Relevance for the Church in Africa," *Missionalia* 1 (1973), pp. 103-111.

[128] See D. N. Freedman and S. Dolansky Overton, "Omitting the Omissions: The Case for Haplography in the Transmission of the Biblical Texts," in *'Imagining' Biblical Worlds: Spatial, Social and Historical Constructs. Essays in Honor of James W. Flanagan*, eds. D. M. Gunn and P. M. McNutt (Sheffield: 2002), pp. 88-105.

[129] Jeffers, *Magic and Divination in Ancient Palestine and Syria*, p. 71.

[130] J. J. Finkelstein, "Hebrew *ḥbr* and Semitic *ḤBR*," *JBL* 75 (1956), suggests that this Hebrew term derives from a different Akkadian word, *ḥabarum*, and he translates Hebrew *ḥbr* accordingly as "to be noisy (in the sense of indistinguishable clamor), to make an uproar" (pp. 329-30). As J. Kuemmerlin-McLean points out, however, "Because Finkelstein does not appeal to any Akkadian uses of the root in a magical context, it is difficult to support any direct transference" (85). Isa 8:19 might indicate, however, that the root *ḥbr* did become associated with muttering in association with the sound made by those reciting spells.

tice of tying magical threads or knots around objects or people,[131] but the exact nature of the practice remains unclear; are the spirits or gods being bound,[132] or is the bound thing or person the object of the spell?[133]

The remaining terms are all associated with necromancy. The precise translation of *šō'ēl 'ôb wĕyiddĕ'ōnî* is less clear than the *dōrēš 'el-hammētîm*, but they both seem to be terms for one who consults the dead for the purposes of augury or divination. The word *'ôb* has a variety of possible etymological derivations.[134] It appears in the context of mourning rites in Leviticus 19, capital sex offenses in Leviticus 20, apostasy in 2 Kings 21, and a judgment oracle in Isa 29:4. In 1 Samuel 28, consulting a woman who has an *'ôb wĕyiddĕ'ōnî* is a last resort for King Saul when Yahweh refuses to answer his questions by the usual (and legal) means of divination. What the *'ôb* itself is, is highly debatable, but most agree that within the Hebrew Bible it can refer to the ritual pit used by the necromancer, the spirit conjured by the necromancer, and the necromancer himself or herself.[135]

Although the word *'ôb* often appears on its own, *yiddĕ'ōnî* is found only in conjunction with *'ôb*, which may indicate that the phrase is a hendiadys,[136] but most scholars argue that each term relates to a separate idea, function, or person.[137] Based on the root *yd'*, this term seems to indicate a "knowing" spirit, presumably the one of whom the necromancer inquires.[138]

---

[131] M. Fishbane, *Studies in Biblical Magic* (diss. Brandeis 1971), pp. 48-133.

[132] Davies suggests this, p. 55.

[133] D. H. Engelhard, "Hittite Magical Practices: An Analysis" (diss, Brandeis, 1970, pp. 136-40) argues for this on the basis of Hittite sources.

[134] See R. E. Friedman and S. Dolansky Overton, "Death and Afterlife: The Biblical Silence," *Judaism in Late Antiquity Part 4: Death, Life-After-Death, Resurrection and The World-to-Come in the Judaisms of Antiquity*, eds. A. J. Avery-Peck and J. Neusner (Leiden: Brill, 1999), p. 44.

[135] See Kuemmerlin-McLean pp. 86-89 for an extended discussion. Based on linguistic grounds as well as the mechanics of necromancy in cross-cultural data, Seidel agrees that the *'ôb* is "indicative of both the spirit raised and the mechanism or site of the raising" (36).

[136] So Davies, pp. 88-89. Jeffers agrees that it is "reasonable to consider these two terms as synonymous" (172).

[137] RSV has "medium and wizard," for example. Seidel agrees that "It makes sense to see the *yiddĕ'ōnî* as either a 'familiar' or another type of ghost, whether or not the *'ôb* is a location, image or ghost" (p. 45).

[138] KBL (367) has "familiar spirit," and Driver translates this way as well (226).

The *ʾôb wĕyiddĕʿōnî* are followed by the last practitioner in the Law Code's list, the *dōrēš ʾel-hammētîm*. This last term is the most obvious reference to a necromancer; the only question it raises is if there is a difference between a *dōrēš ʾel-hammētîm* and a *šōʾēl ʾôb wĕyiddĕʿōnî*. They appear to be two terms for the same occupation, although perhaps they differ in the mechanism or techniques involved.

Presumably, the Law Code's acquaintance with such a variety of magical and divinatory specialists indicates that mantic practices did exist in ancient Israel. As we will see, other texts, in particular the prophets and 1 Samuel 28, corroborate the existence of magic and divination in Israel. Thus the question of why the Law Code prohibits these practices is an important one. First, what is specifically banned? With the possible exception of *mĕkaššēp*, all of the terms refer to divinatory, oracular practices rather than magical or supernatural actions, such as those familiar from Moses and Elijah. What the Law Code prohibits, then, is any possible means of accessing the divine will outside of prophecy. This is underscored by the fact that the larger context of Deuteronomy 18 presents prophets as Israel's legitimate instruments to determining the divine will, as alternatives to the variety of diviners listed in vv 10-11.[139]

There are some important differences between legislation regarding magic in the Holiness Code and what we have seen in the Law Code. Leviticus 19-20 lists fewer magical practices, and they appear in a different context than the Deuteronomy 18 prohibitions. In Leviticus it is not the practitioners but the practices   that are forbidden: *lōʾ tĕnaḥăšû wĕlōʾ tĕʿônēnû ... ʾal-tipnû ʾel-hāʾōbōt wĕʾel- hayiddĕʿōnîm* (Lev 19:26-31). And in Lev 20:6 a punishment for offenders who turn to the *ʾōbōt wĕyiddĕʿōnîm* is made explicit: *kārēt*.[140] On the other hand, in Deut 18:10-11 the list is a cohesive unit in which all of the forbidden practices are magical or divinatory in nature, and no punishments are proposed. In Lev 19 and 20 the context is a variety of other, apparently unrelated,[141] illegal activities: eating blood;[142] cutting hair, beard, and skin; prostitution and other sex crimes.

---

[139] Note, however, Kuemmerlin-McLean's argument that elsewhere Deuteronomy is not generally sympathetic to prophets and "ultimately shifts its focus of revelation and authority from reliance on a person in the present to reliance on a codified tradition from the past" (129). In other words, the most valid source for understanding the present or predicting the future is not a person at all but rather the text of Deuteronomy itself.

[140] Lev 20:27 demands death by stoning for the same offense.

[141] It is difficult to connect all of these different laws by a single overarching theme (see n. 47), but it should be noted that the law in Exod 22:17 condemning the *mĕkaššēpāh* is in a similar context of laws relating to sex crimes and the persecution of aliens.

[142] Kuemmerlin-McLean favors the LXX version which has instead a prohibition against eating "on the mountains," reading *hrm* instead of *hdm*. She ties this to mourning practices

What both legal texts share is a ban on laypeople accessing the realm of the divine. The Law Code explicitly offers legitimate alternatives to divination in the activities of Israelite prophets. It explains that such mantic practices were the activities of other nations, and that performance of such activities was among the things that led to Yahweh's dispossessing those other nations and giving their land to the Israelites in the first place. And in fact, all of the practices and practitioners listed in Deut 18:10-11 have parallels in activities and specialists of Israel's neighbors. The Law Code seems genuinely interested in prohibiting access to any supernatural realm outside of Yahweh.

Likewise, the laws in Leviticus with respect to magic and divination "are clearly placing social markers around acceptable access to otherworldly information,"[143] but the distinction between what laypeople do (forbidden activities such as necromancy) and what priests do is implicit. "In [Lev] 19:31 the illicit oracular seeking 'pollutes' the realm of the sacred because it is a political threat to what is now considered legitimate priestly divination."[144] With respect to divination, the Holiness Code is even stricter and more limiting than the Law Code, which allows for prophecy as a legal alternative to necromancy and other divination or magic. In Leviticus, no alternatives are offered, and the techniques by which non-priests (even other Levites) might access the supernatural are punishable by *kārēt* or even death by stoning, and are grouped with other socially dangerous and reprehensible acts deserving the same strict reprisals.

Thus it would seem that prohibitions against magic and divination in legal materials are concerned with specific activities that are: a) not performed by qualified personnel (prophets in the case of the Law Code, and priests in the Holiness Code); and/or b) seek assistance or information from supernatural entities or powers outside of Yahweh. What is *not* being condemned here, or anywhere else, is the performance of supernatural activities or the acquisition of information from metaphysical realms; in other words, *magic and divination as categories in the modern sense, are not illegal in the Hebrew Bible.* The laws of Deuteronomy 18 and Leviticus 19-20 are solely concerned with limiting access

---

"some of which seem to be general magical and divinatory practices … some of which are closely associated with the spirits of the dead" (140). It is indeed possible to link this as well as laws against cutting hair, skin, and beard, to funerary practices and thus make Lev 19 a more thematically cohesive unit, but this still does not explain why the law against prostituting one's daughter is found in Lev 19:29, or commanding the observation of the Sabbath is in v 30. Then there are the laws about showing respect to the elderly, loving the foreigner, acting justly in measurements, cursing one's parents, committing adultery or incest, homosexuality, and bestiality that all appear in Lev 20:1-26 (around the *'ôb wĕyiddĕ'ōnî* prohibition in v 6) prior to the reiterated censure of a person who has *'ôb 'ô yiddĕ'ōnî* in v 27. It is very difficult to understand Leviticus 19-20 as containing anything other than a variety of thematically unrelated laws and commandments.

[143] Seidel, "Studies in Ancient Jewish Magic," pp. 63-64.

[144] Seidel, "Studies in Ancient Jewish Magic," pp. 63-64.

to such activities and information to qualified people in the Israelite community. Bearing out this distinction are several portrayals of magic and divination in the Hebrew Bible that employ the same vocabulary as the legal texts. These stories demonstrate the efficacy of magic and divination as well as Yahweh's apparent lack of condemnation of it in some instances.

Specialized terms in non-legal materials

Many of the terms found in Deuteronomy and Leviticus appear in prophetic materials. While Isaiah himself is credited with magical abilities (2 Kgs 20:9-11 / Isa 38:7-8),[145] he condemns those who turn to *ʾôb wĕyiddĕʿōnî* (8:19), the *nĕbôn lāḥaš* (3:3), *hallĕḥāšîm* (3:20) and *laḥaš* in general (26:16), the *bĕnê ʿônĕnāh* (57:3) and the *ḥăkam ḥărāšîm* (3:3). This last phrase is the only one not familiar from the legal materials, and in fact the word *ḥărāšîm* occurs only once in this form in the Bible. Based on Aramaic, Arabic and Ugaritic cognates,[146] Jeffers follows Robertson Smith[147] and translates *ḥăkam ḥărāšîm* as "medicine men." Other prophets condemn magic specialties that are more familiar from the legal materials, such as *mĕkaššĕpîm* (Mal 3:5), *qesem* (Mic 3:6-7) and *qōsĕmîm* (Ezek 22:28).

As in the legal literature, however, the prophets do not condemn all magic or all divination, as we can see by their use of the same specialty terms listed in Deuteronomy and Leviticus. Ezekiel even claims that certain outlawed methods of divination work. In 21:26, Ezekiel describes the king of Babylon standing at a crossroads, *"liqsom-qāsem qilqāl baḥiṣṣîm šāʾal battĕrāpîm rāʾāh bakkābēd."* The four different types of divination described here, *qsm*, the shooting of arrows, the inquiring of *tĕrāpîm*,[148] and the examination of the liver, direct Nebuchadnezzar toward Jerusalem rather than to Rabbah in Ammon. In v 28, Ezekiel prophesies that the Judahites will not believe this divination, it will be like a *qĕsom-šāw'* in their eyes, to their detriment. Ezekiel, himself a priest, here describes foreign divination at work in identifying the will of Yahweh, and heaps scorn on the Judahites *for not believing in this divination*.

There are other examples of non-Israelites successfully performing magic or divination in the Bible. As in the example from the book of Ezekiel, at times Yahweh is even explicitly involved in the success of the non-Israelites' super-

---

[145] See discussion in Chapter Three.

[146] See Jeffers, *Magic and Divination in Ancient Palestine and Syria,* p. 49.

[147] Robertson Smith (1884), 124f. He bases this translation on the Arabic root *ḥrš,* meaning medicinal broth, and also sees Aramaic *ḥrš* as equivalent to *mĕkaššĕpîm.*

[148] See discussion below, p. 73ff.

natural activities. The story of Balaam in Numbers 22-24 demonstrates that gifted individuals could discern the will of Yahweh without any intermediation from Israelite priests or prophets. In Numbers 22, Balaam is asked by Balak, king of the Moabites, to *qābāh*, execrate, the Israelite people for him, and in Num 24:1 we are told that he often went *liqra't nĕḥāšîm*. He is a professional diviner and curser, with the power to perform magical execrations. He also is able to converse with his donkey when Yahweh puts words in the beast's mouth (22:28ff). What he is unable to do is Balak's will because Yahweh will not allow him to execrate Israel: "*māh 'eqqōb lō' qabbōh 'ēl / umāh ' ēzōm lō' zāam yhwh?*" (23:8). And further, "*kî lō'-naḥaš bĕyàăqōb / wĕlō'-qesem bĕyisrā'ēl*" (23:23). The point of this story is that even a foreigner who himself has magical powers, a) is subject to the will of Yahweh, and b) bears witness to the greatness of Israel. There is no condemnation of his magical powers; they are stated neutrally in the text, and ultimately result in positive consequences for Israel.

Likewise, the story in 1 Samuel 5-6 of the Philistines' capture of the ark of Yahweh demonstrates the efficacy of both magic and divination for Israel's neighbors. The Philistines are plagued by mice and by hemorrhoids because they have taken the ark captive. Desperate, they turn to their priests and their *qōsĕmîm* to determine the proper way to return the ark and put an end to these plagues (6:2). The priests and *qōsĕmîm* recommend an act of sympathetic magic: models of the mice and the hemorrhoids that plague the Philistine people should be made of gold and sent back to Israel along with the ark. The Philistines do this and are relieved of both plagues. Thus the divination proves correct and the magic successful.

It is possible that these cases of successful and ultimately positive magic and divination on the part of foreign specialists would not have been problematic for those who condemn such magic and divination within biblical materials, such as Leviticus and Deuteronomy. In both cases, the legal literature makes clear that such activities are not acceptable for *Israelites*. They do not claim that the techniques they prohibit are ineffective. Rather, they are dangerous *because they work*, and thus allow laypeople to circumvent priestly intermediation, threatening the very livelihood of the landless priests who depend on the offering of sacrifices in order to survive.

The episode involving the woman at En-Dor who has *'ôb wĕyiddĕ'ōnî* in 1 Samuel 28 demonstrates both the illegality of such practices within Israel and their ultimate effectiveness. The text itself states that when Yahweh will not answer Saul by the usual (legal) methods of divination, Saul asks that a *bàalat-'ôb* be found so that he might inquire (*drš*) of her. It is explicit that the normal means for an Israelite king to determine his course of action during a crisis situation, in this case a war with the Philistines, consist of inquiring of Yahweh (v 6) *baḥălōmôt ... bā' ûrîm ... bannĕbî'îm*. When these royal, priestly, and prophetic methods of divination fail, Saul finds another unofficial way to acquire supernatural guidance. In v 3 we are told he had banished the *'ōbôt* wĕ'et-hayyiddĕʿōnîm from the land. However, a servant of Saul's finds one at En-Dor at the king's request. Saul disguises himself and goes to her, asking her to qosŏmî-nā' lî bā' ôb wĕhaʿălî lî 'ēt 'ăšer-'ōmar 'ēlâyik (v 8). The woman successfully raises the deceased prophet Samuel who has an abundance of bad news for the beleaguered king, bad news that the following day comes true to the letter.

Thus, the story of Saul and the woman of En-Dor involves both magic (the conjuring of the deceased Samuel) and divination (the dead prophet predicts the future), and demonstrates two main points. First, it shows that divination via necromancy is a viable (albeit illegal) alternative to official royal, priestly, and prophetic means of determining the divine will. The fact that it is illegal and that Saul himself had made it so does not mean that it does not work. On the contrary; it works quite well. The second point is precisely that it works so well and yet does not need to involve either cult officials *or* Yahweh himself. These are two perfectly good reasons why priests would declare such a practice illegal, threatening kārēt or death for those who violate this law.[149]

As we have seen, terminology from Deuteronomy 18 and Leviticus 19-20 appears also in non-legal materials, which help clarify the nature and purpose of the priestly prohibitions. Conversely, some terms that relate to magic and divination appear only outside of the materials condemning the specialties discussed above. The words 'ēpôd, 'ûrîm, tummîm, and tĕrāpîm all refer not to practitioners or specialists but rather to mantic devices that are legitimate within the Israelite cult. This is why they are not included in Deuteronomy 18 or Leviticus 19-20.

It is difficult to determine exactly what the ephod was.[150] In some texts it is a garment of linen[151] worn by priests.[152] Other passages suggest its use as a divinatory tool,[153] perhaps a function of the garment,[154], although some scholars posit that the same word is applied to two separate objects, an item of clothing

---

[149] The woman of En-Dor indicates that death is the penalty Saul himself has imposed on necromancers when she asks the disguised Saul (v 9), wĕlâmāh 'attâh mitnāqqēš bĕnāpšî lāhămîtênî?

[150] For an extensive bibliography on the subject, see I. Friedrich, *Ephod und Choschen im Lichte des Alten Orients* (Wien: Herder, 1968) pp. 10-12. For possible etymological derivations of the word, see Jeffers pp. 203-4.

[151] 1 Sam 2:18; 2 Sam 6:14.

[152] Exod 25:7; 28:4-8; 35:9, 27; 39:1-7, 20-26.

[153] 1 Sam 23:9-13; 30:7-8 (half of v 7 is missing in the Greek, but this does not affect the meaning or implication of divination in this passage).

[154] Davies suggests this (p. 119).

and a portable image or idol.[155]   Several of the biblical contexts of this word
indicate an oracular function for the ephod. As   C. Meyers indicates, a likely
solution to the nature of the ephod is that it is the garment to which the *ʾûrîm* and
tummîm are attached, and thus the divinatory nature of the garment derives from
this.[156]   David consults the ephod in 1 Samuel 23 when he seeks an indication
from Yahweh regarding the outcome of a battle, and it is the priest Ahijah who
brings the ephod before David.   In 1 Samuel 30, David inquires of Yahweh by
means of the ephod again, seeking advice regarding strategy in his fight with the
Amalekites.   This positive use of the ephod by David and his high priest contrasts sharply with the condemnation of Gideon's ephod in Judg 8:27, perhaps
because this one is made available for laypeople to use.   In Judg 17:5, an ephod
and teraphim are mentioned along with "the graven image" and "the molten image" (Judg 18:17) that are part of Micah's shrine, and the Levite who officiated
as a priest for Micah was asked to inquire of Yahweh on behalf of the Danites
(18:5).   The ephod is likewise paired with teraphim in Hos 3:4 in a context
which implies the acceptability of both instruments.

     Like the ephod, it is difficult to determine either what the teraphim were or
their legitimacy in the Israelite cult. The etymology of the term suggests an origin in Hittite *tarpis*, "spirit,"[157] and they were likely ancestor figurines used in
both private and public contexts for divination.[158]   Their use by the king of
Babylon in Ezekiel 21 as one of his means of divining his path demonstrates
their oracular function.   Their status in Israelite religion is more difficult to as-
sess.   In 2 Kings 23:24, they are removed by Josiah along with *hāʾōbôt,*
hayyiddĕʿōnîm, and *haggillūlîm.* In 1 Sam 15:23, Samuel categorizes the use of
tĕrāpîm along with the sin of *qesem.* Zech 10:2 likewise condemns them along
with *qōsĕmîm.* However, in Judges 17-18 we learn that, along with the ephod,
teraphim could be used by a priest as part of the instruments of a shrine.   And in
Hos 3:4 their legitimacy is implied by the context in which they are mentioned.

     The *ʾûrîm* and *tummîm* are more clearly legitimate oracular instruments
within the Israelite cult.   Exod 28:2ff and Leviticus 8 indicate that they were
small enough to be kept within the high priest's breastplate.   The verbs used in

---

[155] See Jeffers, *Magic and Divination in Ancient Palestine and Syria,* pp. 202-3.

[156] "The ephod was both a special garment and a ritual object, and in either or both of these
aspects it functioned symbolically to bring a human representative of the Israelite community
into contact with the unseen God" ("Ephod," C. Meyers, *Anchor Bible Dictionary*).

[157] H. A. Hoffner, Jr., "Hittite tarpis and Hebrew teraphim," *JNES* 27 (1968), pp. 61-68.

[158] K. Van der Toorn, "The Nature of Biblical Teraphim in the Light of Cuneiform Evi-
dence," *CBQ* 52 (1990), p. 211. For their relation to Israelite ancestor veneration, see R. E.
Friedman and S. Dolansky Overton, "Death and Afterlife: The Biblical Silence," *Judaism in
Late Antiquity Part 4: Death, Life-After-Death, Resurrection and The World-to-Come in the
Judaisms of Antiquity,* eds. A. J. Avery-Peck and J. Neusner (Leiden: Brill, 1999), pp. 42-43.

connection with them suggest that they were stones or dice that could indicate three possible answers to questions put by the high priest: positive, negative, or no response (Num 27:21; 1 Sam 14:36). They could also be used to make a selection between two choices (1 Sam 14:41). Many suggestions regarding their nature have been put forward,[159] and most agree that they were a form of cleromancy, the casting of lots. A number of texts demonstrate the legitimacy of this form of divination in the hands of priests. They are kept in the high priest's breastplate (Lev 8:8), and according to Deut 33:8 their existence can be traced back to Moses. Moses could communicate directly with Yahweh (Num 12:6-8), but his successors could not. Joshua must inquire of the deity by means of the *ûrîm* and *tummîm* wielded by the high priest on his behalf (Num 27:21). Likewise, the *ûrîm* are included in the list of legitimate means by which King Saul expected to obtain an oracle from Yahweh in 1 Sam 28:6.

In the pre- and post-monarchic periods there were other valid forms of cleromancy in use in ancient Israel.[160] Joshua uses lots to determine Achan's guilt in stealing proscribed goods (Josh 7:16-21) as well as to assign territorial divisions to the tribes (Joshua 18-21). Lots were also employed to decide who would avenge the death of the Levite's concubine in Gibeah (Judges 20). In 1 Chronicles 24-26 and Neh 10:35, lots determined the assignment of duties among priests and Levites. And in the first chapter of the book of Jonah the sailors use lots to find out that the cause of God's displeasure is Jonah, and throw him overboard as a result (Jonah 1:7).

The Bible has two other words that refer to magicians and magical practices that do not occur in legal texts or prophetic works. Rather, these words are used repeatedly in narrative contexts but only of foreign magicians. The most common and most general term for foreign magician in the Bible is *ḥartōm*,[161] a Hebrew word likely derived from Egyptian *ḥry-tp*, "lector priest, magician."[162]

---

[159] See especially Jeffers, pp. 209-212. An explanation from D. N. Freedman (private communication) is that they were a pair of dice marked with *ʾālēp* and *tāw*. When both came up *ʾālēp* the answer was negative, both *tāw* indicated a positive response from the deity. One of each meant no response.

[160] See S. A. Nigosian, "Anti-Divinatory Statements in Biblical Codes," *Theological Review* XVIII/1, 1997, pp. 21-34; J. Lindblom, "Lot-casting in the Old Testament," *VT* 12 (1962), pp. 164-178; H. B. Huffmon, "Priestly Divination in Israel," in *The Word of the Lord Shall Go Forth*, ed. C. Meyers and M. O'Connor (Winona Lake: Eisenbrauns, 1983), pp. 355-358.

[161] Forms of this word occur in Gen 41:8, 24; Exod 7:11, 22; 8:3, 14, 15; 9:11; Dan 1:20; 2:2, 10, 27; 4:4, 6, 11, 15.

[162] A. S. Yahuda, *The Language of the Pentateuch in Its Relation to Egyptian* (London, 1933), pp. 93-94; J. Quaegebeur, "On the Egyptian Equivalent of Biblical *ḥartummîm*," in S. Israelit-Groll, ed., *Pharaonic Egypt, the Bible, and Christianity* (Jerusalem, 1985), pp. 162-72; S. Noegel, "Moses and Magic: Notes on the Book of Exodus" *JANES* 24 (1996), pp. 45-59; and J. Vergote, "Joseph in Egypt," *Orientalia et Biblica Lovaniensia* 3 (1959) pp. 66-73.

In Genesis and Exodus, *ḥarṭōm* is the label applied to Pharaoh's magicians in the context of Joseph's sojourn in Egypt, in the accounts of Aaron's rod becoming a snake, and in three of the ten plagues. The word does not occur again until the book of Daniel, when it is applied to Babylonian magicians along with the term *'āšēp*.[163] The *'āšĕpîn* of the Babylonian court accompany the *ḥakkîmîn* and the *ḥarṭummîn* when summoned by the king to interpret his dreams and the mysterious writing on the wall. Interestingly, the word *'āšēp* is used only of Babylonian magicians and itself derives from Akkadian *āšipu*, "exorcist."[164]

There are two things worth noting about the use of these words. First, the description of the Egyptian magicians as *ḥarṭummîm* may denote some familiarity on the part of the author(s) with Egyptian magical practice and terminology.[165] It is significant that this originally Egyptian word is used only of Egyptian magicians everywhere in the Bible except for the book of Daniel. Presumably by the time of the composition of Daniel the word denoted "magician" in general, as the specific etymology and origin of the word would have long been lost. Likewise, the use of an Akkadian loanword *'āšēp* to describe another type of Babylonian magician that might be found around Nebuchadnezzar's palace might demonstrate some knowledge of Babylonian magical practice on the part of the author of Daniel.

The second significant point about the use of these two words is that, although the most common terms for "magician" in the Bible, they are not listed in either Deuteronomy 18 or Leviticus 19-20. The key to understanding the reason for this lies in the narrative passages in which the terms appear. The words denote only non-Israelite magicians, *even when Israelites demonstrate the same capabilities.* Joseph is able to perform the task that the *ḥăkāmîm* and *ḥarṭummîm* are usually able to do for Pharaoh but in this case cannot. Although Pharaoh calls Joseph *ḥākām* in Gen 41:39, no one ever calls him a *ḥarṭōm*. Even more striking are the episodes involving Moses and Aaron. In Exodus 7, Aaron turns a rod into a *tannîn*, and the Egyptian *ḥarṭummîm* do the same. Aaron proves the more powerful, however, as his serpent devours those of the Egyptians. In Exodus 7 and 8, two of the plagues brought on by Moses and Aaron are replicated by Egyptian *ḥarṭummîm*. In other words, Moses and Aaron can perform the same wonders as the *ḥarṭummîm*, yet neither Egyptians nor Israelites ever refer

---

Both BDB (355) and KBL (333) propose an etymology based on the Hebrew word *ḥereṭ* (chisel), and S. Parpola, in *Letters from Assyrian Scholars to the Kings Esarhaddon and Assurbanipal* (Neukirchen/Vluyn: Kevelaer, 1971) suggests a derivation from Akkadian *ḥarṭibi* which he translates as "interpreters of dreams."

[163] Forms of this word occur in Dan 1:20, 2:2, 10, 27, 4:4, 5:11.

[164] CAD, vol. 1, part 2, p. 41; S. Parpola (1971).

[165] On this subject, see the excellent article by S. Noegel cited in n 66.

to them as *ḥarṭummîm* – even though this would seem to be the obvious title for such a worker of magic in this context.

In fact, no special terms are applied to Moses and Aaron here, or to their supernatural activities. This makes Exodus 7 and 8 something different from the previous stories that we have examined in which magic appears. The fact that Moses and Aaron are practicing magic is only implicit in the text in the designation of the Egyptian experts who conduct the same activities as *ḥarṭummîm*. The author here is trying to show that Moses and Aaron, with Yahweh's backing, are more powerful than the Egyptians, their Pharaoh, or their gods, and he is doing so in explicitly Egyptian terms. The exclamation by the Egyptian magicians in 8:15 that "this is the finger of God" shows the extent to which the Priestly author is walking a tightrope. To an Israelite audience, this statement could indicate the foreigners' acknowledgment that the power being demonstrated by Moses has a higher and supremely powerful source. In the Egyptian context, however, the attribution of magical events to "the finger of [a god]" occurs frequently in magic literature in connection with a god's patronage of magic.[166] Thus the author demonstrates the power of Moses and Aaron within an Egyptian context, but is trying to show that what they are doing is somehow different. It is Yahweh who is acting through them, even if the actions initially appear to be the same as those of the *ḥarṭummîm*.

Biblical Perspectives on Magic

In examining a variety of explicit depictions of magic and related activities in the Hebrew Bible, we have been looking at laws, stories, and prophetic pronouncements in which a rich and detailed vocabulary is employed. The Bible uses words like *ḥarṭōm* and *ʾāšēp* that specifically refer to foreign magicians, described in neutral terms, in narrative contexts. They are never condemned, nor is the claim ever made that they are ineffective; rather they are depicted as less powerful only in the face of a contest with a champion of Yahweh.

The Bible also uses a variety of different words and phrases for magical and divinatory practices and practitioners within Israel. Analysis of the etymologies of these terms reveals that they were activities shared by many of Israel's neighbors. Whether they originated within Israel or as a result of foreign influence, they are rife in Israel from the time of Saul through the destruction of the kingdoms, according to several narrative and prophetic works. Deuteronomy 18 condemns such activities on the grounds that they are originally foreign to Israel and that Israel has its own legitimate alternative for determining the

---

[166] See S. Noegel, "Moses and Magic"; also A. S. Yahuda, *The Language of the Pentateuch*, pp.66-67.

divine will in the institution of prophecy. Leviticus 19-20 prohibit some of the practices mentioned in Deuteronomy, grouping them with other social taboos, prescribes both the death penalty and *kārēt* for engaging in such practices, and, unlike Deuteronomy, offer no explanation for their condemnation.

The legal literature, in conjunction particularly with the details provided in 1 Samuel 28, strongly suggests that the authors of priestly materials such as the Law Code and the Holiness Code have a very good reason for prohibiting mantic activities among laypeople: fear of competition. Divination is legal if performed by priests with *'ûrîm* and *tummîm*, or by means of prophecy. It is illegal when performed by other people, by other means. The priests will accept competition only from prophets[167] and fear all other mantic specialists precisely because what they do *works*. It works without priests, and it even works without Yahweh. Thus, it is a serious threat on the one hand to the livelihood of the priests and to the monotheistic impulse of their official religion, and on the other hand to the legitimacy and status of prophets, often found in or affiliated with the royal court.

Thus, contrary to most scholarship on the issue of the Hebrew Bible's stance toward magic, magic itself is not categorically condemned. Only certain lay specialists are actually prohibited, and only in the legal and some prophetic materials. Other prophetic and some narrative texts demonstrate that these specialists continued to operate in Israel and that their methods were believed to have worked. Most scholars view the biblical attitude toward magic and divination only through the lens of Deuteronomy 18 and Leviticus 19-20 and assume that the specialties listed in these texts constitute the entire category of magic. A closer look has demonstrated that this is not the case.

As we shall see in the next chapter, there are many more stories involving Israelites who use magic. The difference is that in those cases none of the special terms we have discussed are applied. In this chapter we have gained an understanding of what magic constituted in the minds of the Israelites and the authors of the Bible. The conclusions that we carry into the next chapter are, first, that magic and divination are not categorically condemned in the Hebrew Bible. Second, it is the priestly legal codes that prohibit the practice of magic on the part of laypeople. This opens up two possible subjects for inquiry. First, the magic that the priests themselves practiced. Second, the magic that non-priests practiced or wrote about despite the legal prohibitions. Interestingly, in these cases, none of the terms for practices the priests declared illegal are employed.

The difficulty of this task lies in the lack of terminology that readily identifies a particular passage in the Bible as discussing magic. In all of the cases we

---

[167] The Holiness Code does not even mention prophets, and although Deuteronomy presents prophets as a viable alternative to divination and magic, Deut 13:1-6 as well as Deuteronomy 18 strongly caution against the possibility of false prophets.

examined in this chapter, such terms as are found in the legal literature helped determine cases in which magic and/or divination was performed. In investigating these cases we came to an understanding of how the Bible itself identifies magic. Establishing a precise definition is challenging, because the practices of magicians and diviners have clear parallels and in fact overlap with the official activities of the religious leaders of the Israelite cult. The implicit biblical idea of magic seems to be very close to the definition we provided in Chapter One above: the manipulation of supernatural forces, with or without attribution to Yahweh, including the ability to gain information concerning the divine will and/or future events. We will apply this biblical sense of what constitutes magic, as well as our earlier definition, to the rest of the biblical text to determine cases of the practice of magic in which special terminology is not employed, in the following chapter.

Chapter Three

Magic: For Prophet?

Prophecy and Magic

As we saw in the previous chapter, despite prohibitions on laypeople accessing the divine realm for power or information, divination and magic did exist in ancient Israel. The illegal specialties listed in Deuteronomy 18 and Leviticus 19-20 constituted different forms of divination and magic that were officially condemned. But the fact that they were subject to condemnation means that they existed and that a contemporary audience would have been familiar with them. In addition, there were other ways in which the divine will could legitimately be accessed, even if the terms found in the legal literature do not apply. In fact, as we will see, magic is at the heart of Israelite myth and religion. The magic wielded by priests and prophets is essential in the cult, worldview, and historical consciousness of ancient Israelite society.

In the last chapter we discussed several instances of legitimate forms of divination described in biblical stories. For example, in pre-monarchic times, lot-casting was a frequent method of allowing Yahweh to decide an important issue. Under the monarchy, priests divined God's will by means of the *'ûrîm* and *tummîm* or the *'ēpôd*. The most common and characteristic form of divination in ancient Israel, however, was not practiced by priests but rather by gifted individuals who were "called" to the position of a prophet. If divination is "a technique of communication with the supernatural forces that are supposed to shape the history of the individual as well as the group,"[168] prophecy certainly falls under this category.

The goal of prophecy and divination is the same: to facilitate communication between God and Israel. As a result, the line between prophecy and divination is often obscured. As L. L. Grabbe notes, "One might formally distinguish spontaneous prophetic revelation from spirit divination, in which the answer to a specific question is sought. But the modes of revelation are often the same, and it is clear that at least some prophecies in the OT are said to be the result of divine inquiry."[169]

---

[168] A. L. Oppenheim, *Ancient Mesopotamia* (Chicago: University of Chicago Press, 1964), p. 207.

[169] L. L. Grabbe, *Priests, Prophets, Diviners, Sages: A Socio-Historical Study of Religious Specialists in Ancient Israel* (Pennsylvania: Trinity Press, 1995), pp. 150-151.

The writing prophets themselves seem to have differing opinions on how to distinguish true prophecy from *qesem*. Jeremiah links false prophecy with *qesem* in 14:14 and 27:9, and Second Isaiah also contrasts divination with prophecy in Isa 44:25. But in Mic 3:6-8, prophecy and divination seem to be the same thing, and God will answer neither prophets nor diviners. Only Micah will receive messages from Yahweh. In v 11, an activity of some prophets is actually called *qesem*, and Micah's condemnation of them is not for committing *qesem* but rather for doing so for pay. And Isa 3:2 lists diviners among Judaean warriors, officials, prophets, and elders. As we have already noted, non-Israelites successfully use *qesem* in 1 Sam 6:2 and in Ezek 21:26. In the case of Ezekiel, he prophesies that the Judahites will not believe the divination performed by the king of Babylon; it will be like *qĕsom-šāw'* in their eyes, to their detriment!

Thus in the sources themselves, the line is blurred between the two techniques for producing oracles. For some prophets, *qesem* is prophecy's antithesis[170]; for others, prophecy is understood to be a legal form of *qesem*.[171] This is because prophecy and *qesem* are different paths toward the same outcome: the receipt of a divine oracle. For the Deuteronomist, the Israelite prophet was "the only legitimate channel of communication between Yahweh and the people,"[172] and as we saw in Chapter Two, he rejects other forms of divination as foreign. This explains why groups promoting prophecy would condemn *qesem*. "The fact that passages criticizing divination are found largely in Deuteronomistic and prophetic contexts suggests that ideology and vested interests had a role to play."[173] Competition between the two groups would be inevitable, and this results in the official ban on *qesem* by priestly and prophetic circles.

Non-Prophet Magicians

Several figures in the Bible who are neither priests nor prophets also perform magical acts. They are, however, all men with whom God communicates regularly. Thus even in the absence of the official title "prophet," they are "men of God" and as such seem able to exhibit Yahweh's power.

---

[170] In addition to Jeremiah 14:14, see 1 Sam 15:23.

[171] Mic 3:6-8, 11, as noted above.

[172] R. R. Wilson, *Prophecy and Society in Ancient Israel* (Philadelphia: Fortress Press, 1980), p. 162.

[173] T. Overholt, *Channels of Prophecy: The Social Dynamics of Prophetic Activity* (Minneapolis: Fortress Press, 1989), p. 126.

In traditions attributed to both J and E, there are two figures in Genesis who stand out for their apparent magical and/or divinatory capabilities. In E, Joseph's ability as an oneiromancer is in fact what promotes his governmental career in Egypt. His father Jacob, in the J text, performs the only example of a possibly magical act in the book of Genesis. In the difficult text of Gen 30:31-43, Jacob manages to alter the genetic patterns of his father-in-law Laban's flocks in such a way that the stronger animals would be speckled and spotted and therefore belong to him, while the weaker animals would remain Laban's. Yet its qualification as an act of magic is unclear and has recently been disputed by S. Noegel.[174] He argues against the majority of scholars, who see the super-natural at work in this passage,[175] that the mysterious poplar rods that Jacob erects at the watering trough are not magical instruments but rather a type of "*phallus fallax,*" and that "Jacob allowed only the animals which he did not want to sire offspring to 'become heated upon the rods.'"[176] This provides a physical, causal explanation for the proliferation of strong animals in Jacob's own flock and the weakening of Laban's flock, and eliminates the magical qual-ity from this strange breeding practice. It should, however, be noted that this passage is far from clear in its wording[177] and has been traditionally understood as referring to a magical manipulation of the flocks' breeding patterns.[178] The question of whether or not an Israelite audience would have understood this in terms of a common breeding practice or as the manifestation of extraordinary magical intervention is difficult to answer. If the latter, the fact that Jacob ap-pears to initiate the actions and perform the magic himself yet attributes the suc-cessful proliferation of strong animals to Yahweh, fits well with the other bibli-cal stories of "men of God" who wield magic.

---

[174] S. B. Noegel, "Sex, Sticks, and the Trickster in Gen. 30:31-43," *JANES* 25 (1997), pp. 7-17.

[175] For example, R. D. Sack, *A Commentary on the Book of Genesis* (Lewiston, 1990); G. von Rad, *Genesis: A Commentary* (Philadelphia, 1972); and E. M. Good, *Irony in the Old Testament* (Sheffield, 1981).

[176] Noegel, p. 10. Additionally, R. E. Friedman points out the difficulty of ascertaining whether or not an Israelite audience would have understood Jacob's actions as magical, given our lack of knowledge of Israelite notions of heredity (*Commentary on the Torah*, pp. 132-33).

[177] Obscure wording and the unclear usage of prepositions and modifiers all contribute to the difficulty of this passage.

[178] Noegel (pp. 8-9) indicates that Rashi, Ibn Ezra, and Malbim all insert the gloss "at the sight of the rods" in Gen 30:39, and that their glosses can be understood only within the con-text of a medieval belief in fertility-magic that the visual impression perceived by a female at the moment of conception would influence the appearance of her offspring.

Oneiromancy is a well-known divinatory practice throughout the ancient Near East, and there are examples of it in the Bible as well. Genesis 39-41 demonstrate that Joseph has an uncommon gift for prophetic dreaming and extremely accurate dream interpretation. And like the prophets who will follow in later generations, E's Joseph attempts to explain that the interpretations are from God (for example, Gen. 40:8; 41:16), while his audiences continually credit Joseph, the visible agent of Yahweh, instead (Gen. 41:12, 14). Similarly, Daniel is not only a successful oneiromancer (Dan. 1:17; 4:15) but also performs magical feats (Dan. 6:18-24) and acknowledges Yahweh's responsibility for both abilities (Dan. 2:22-23, 28). Thus the actions of Jacob, Joseph, and Daniel all provide visible testimony to the power of the God of Israel. In the cases of Joseph and Daniel, operating within the foreign courts of Egypt, Babylon, and Persia, a foremost purpose of their amazing feats is arguably to demonstrate the power of Yahweh in a manner analogous to Moses and Aaron's actions in Egypt.[179]

The Magic of Prophets

Prophets not only perform the same services as diviners, but they are the only Israelites[180] in biblical narrative who are credited with the performance of magical acts.[181] The wonder-working abilities of some of Israel's prophets definitely fall under the category of "magical" activity. Moses sets the example for all of Yahweh's subsequent messengers: he is the first and greatest of Israel's prophets. The purpose of a prophet in Israel is made explicit in Deuteronomy 18, in the passage immediately following the list of prohibited magical activities examined in Chapter Two above: Yahweh says "I will put my words in his mouth, and he will speak to them everything I command him" (Deut 18:18). The Israelite prophet is to serve as Yahweh's mouthpiece, just like Moses and Aaron at the foundation of the Israelite nation. Because the Israelites find God's voice unbearable, He will address them only through the agency of a prophet

---

[179] For example, see Daniel 2:47 in which, as a result of Daniel's ability to reveal both dream and interpretation to the Babylonian king, Nebuchadnezzar exclaims to Daniel, "In truth your God is the God of gods and the Lord of kings!"

[180] Again, it is not clear whether or not Jacob performs magic. Although he is never labeled a "prophet," he is a person with whom God communicates and therefore well within the pre-Moses tradition of a prophet. For example, Abraham is understood to be a prophet, even if he is only referred to as such on one occasion (Gen 20:7). It could also be argued that Samson performs magic and is not a prophet. He is credited with feats of extraordinary strength, although such acts do not fall under the category of magic as defined herein since there is a physical, causal connection between his actions and the intended result, even if his physical prowess appears to be supernatural.

[181] We are distinguishing the performance of magical "signs and wonders," the provenance of prophets, from the magical *concepts* and *premises* that underlie much of priestly ritual: see Chapter Four.

whom He chooses. The same passage in Deuteronomy is quick to address the obvious problem – how is one to know if a prophet is speaking in Yahweh's name or for another god (in which case he is to be put to death)?[182] In 18:22 we are told simply that if the word spoken by a prophet does not come to be then he was not a prophet of Yahweh.

This was never a satisfactory test for prophets. Even Moses, when God first commissions him to lead the Israelites out of Egypt, protests to God that the people will have no way of knowing that Yahweh has sent him. In response, God gives the first prophet, in his first act of prophecy, three signs by which the people will know that Yahweh has sent him; and in doing so He sets a precedent that other prophets will follow. Despite the statement in Deut 18:22, the presence of a "sign" by which an audience may know that a prophet is true becomes the hallmark of some of Israel's most famous prophets. Deuteronomy 13 anticipates the problem of prophets wielding this kind of magical power when Yahweh says, "When a prophet or one who has a dream will get up among you and will give you a sign or a wonder, and the sign or the wonder of which he spoke to you, saying, 'Let us go after other gods,' whom you have not known, 'and let us serve them' will come to pass, you shall not listen to the words of that prophet or to that one who has the dream, because Yahweh your God is testing you...." (Deut 13:2-4).

Not all prophets produce the kinds of signs and wonders that we would term "magical" in nature. Many signs are symbolic, such as the wearing or breaking of a yoke (Jeremiah 27-28), walking naked through the streets (Isaiah 20[183]; Mic 1:8), eating a scroll (Ezek 3:1-3), or marrying a prostitute (Hos 1:2-3). Some scholars suggest that the purpose of performing such symbolic actions is to magically bring the prophecy to fruition. G. Fohrer argues that the symbolic act consists of the imitation of the expected results and is efficacious due to "the principle of analogy" in such a way that "that which was acted upon in the imitation should also result in the prototype."[184] Although this is an intriguing suggestion that would subsume symbolic acts under our definition of magic, we are focusing as much as possible on what the text seems to indicate. There is no hint in any of these cases that the prophets themselves thought they were *producing* the events they prophesied by performing their symbolic actions. Rather, their actions appear to have been a visual corollary to the verbal messages they were delivering to the Israelites on God's behalf. Within biblical narrative, the delivery of a message is the primary function of Israelite prophets. If they perform magic, it is always in the service of establishing their credentials and Yahweh's power. When prophets do produce magical signs and wonders, it always leads to recognition by the people that these are "men of God." Despite the caution in Deuteronomy 13, in biblical stories magical abili-

---

[182] Deut 18:20.

[183] In Isa 1:20, the prophet's actions are actually referred to as " '*ōt ûmôpēt.*"

[184] G. Fohrer "Prophetie und Magie," *ZAW* 78 (1966), p. 34.

ties are always portrayed as serving to convince the people that a magician is a true agent of Yahweh.

Moses and Aaron

The most complete biography of a prophet with magical powers in the Hebrew Bible is the story of Moses. Moses is neither a prophet nor a wonderworker until he encounters Yahweh at the burning bush. There he is given instructions to speak on God's behalf to the Israelites and to Pharaoh, and his protests are met with the endowment by God of magical powers with which he is to convince the people, and later Pharaoh, of his own authority as well as Yahweh's might. The "signs" that Moses is to display to the people to convince them of his prophetic office are the ability to turn a staff into a snake, to make his own hand "leprous" and then return it to its normal skin tone, and to make water from the Nile become blood on the dry ground. Moses performs these wonders before the people, "and the people believed" (Exod 4:31).

When Moses and Aaron encounter Pharaoh and Aaron turns his rod into a snake, it is still made explicit that Yahweh is behind the magic. He has commanded Moses and Aaron regarding what will happen and what their responses should be every step of the way, and this continues through the plague narrative. It is made clear in the story that God is behind these wonders and that he is orchestrating them; Moses and Aaron are merely his agents. The same pattern is apparent when God instructs Moses to split the Sea in Exodus 14 (and Moses is not even mentioned in the poem of Exodus 15), to sweeten the water at Marah (15:24-5), and to draw water from a rock (17:5-6). When they fight with the Amalekites (17:8-13), however, and Moses' raised staff magically helps Joshua and the Israelites to prevail, Yahweh is not mentioned until after the battle has been won, when Moses builds a commemorative altar in God's name.

The next episode involving Moses and magic occurs in Numbers 16. When Moses' leadership is directly challenged by Korah, Dathan, and Abiram, Moses explicitly calls for a miracle to demonstrate that his authority comes from Yahweh. He says, "By this you will know that Yahweh sent me to do all these things, because it is not from my own heart ... and if Yahweh will create and the ground will open its mouth and swallow them and all that is theirs and they will go down alive to Sheol, then you will know that these people have rejected Yahweh" (16:28-30). As he finishes speaking, the earth opens and swallows the dissenters, their families, and their property. In this text, there is no indication that God has coached Moses through the steps to performing a miracle; Moses himself dictates the miracle, and presumably Yahweh causes it to occur as a result. The function of Moses' supernatural abilities is still to convince the people of his ability to speak in Yahweh's name, as his prophet; his magic is bound up with his prophetic office, for the explicit purpose of demonstrating his authority as Yahweh's messenger. But this story reads differently from the majority of narratives concerning Moses' magic in that Moses does not appear to be merely the agent who carries out Yahweh's instructions; here Moses is portrayed as initiating the magical activities himself, and Yahweh silently complies with Moses' request.

This is an anomaly. It stands out particularly in light of the final three magical episodes in the book of Numbers. In Numbers 17 Aaron's staff blooms, and Yahweh is directly responsible. When the people are attacked by snakes in Numbers 21, Yahweh commands Moses to construct *nĕḥuštān*, the sight of this bronze serpent will instantly cure snake-bite. Most tellingly, in Numbers 20, Moses is directed by Yahweh to bring water out of a rock in what seems to be a parallel account to the Exodus 17 story. In the Numbers version, however, Moses and Aaron are told to speak to the rock so that it will yield its water. Not only does Moses strike the rock with his staff as he had in Exodus 17, but in his anger at the people he seems to forget that he himself does not command the power in his own right to produce the water, asking "Shall *we* bring water from this rock for you?" This one statement will have devastating ramifications. Although the issue of Moses' sin has been much debated, the text seems to indicate the ultimate punishment of not being permitted to enter the Promised Land is a result of Moses ascribing miraculous powers to himself and Aaron, and not to God.[185] Moses has forgotten that he "is only the agent of the supreme God. He is not the initiator of the miraculous but only its executor. He is a prophet."[186]

Moses has come a long way from the simple shepherd who meets God at the burning bush and learns a few magic tricks that will help him convince people that he is a legitimate prophet of Yahweh. By the time of the events described in Numbers 20, the last time that Moses will perform magic in his life, he has forgotten the very thing that has been so carefully portrayed throughout the pentateuchal narratives. A primary purpose of magic in the hands of a prophet is to demonstrate his legitimacy as God's representative, a pattern that is established at the burning bush with the very first prophetic commission in the Bible.

But the question remains: why is Moses punished for assuming responsibility for the miracle of producing water from the rock *here* and not elsewhere? In Exodus 17:8-13, Moses raises his staff on his own initiative, causing Joshua and the Israelites to prevail against the Amalekites. Why is he not punished in this case? For that matter, why is Joshua not punished in Josh 10:12-14 when he commands Yahweh to stop the course of the sun for the duration of his battle with the Amorites? And in the books of Kings, why are Elijah and Elisha so seemingly empowered with magical abilities in their own rights, often without any attribution to Yahweh?

---

[185] J. Milgrom, "Magic, Monotheism and the Sin of Moses," in *The Quest for the Kingdom of God: Studies in Honor of G. E. Mendenhall*, eds. H. B. Huffmon, F. A. Spina, and A. R. W. Green (Indiana: Eisenbrauns, 1983) p. 257.

[186] Milgrom, "Magic, Monotheism and the Sin of Moses," p. 259.

Source Criticism

Attention to the sources of different stories about magic in the Hebrew Bible resolves many of these questions and sheds much light on the issue of who can legitimately wield magic and why. In the Torah, there are differences in the frequency, type, and characterization of magic among the texts of J, E, P, and D. In particular, there are differences in the ways in which J, E, and P portray the magical acts of individuals in parallel stories.

There is much evidence suggesting that P was composed as an alternative to the redacted JE.[187] P follows the order of JE, but promotes priestly interests in laws, the person of Aaron, the tabernacle, and the centralization of sacrifice as the only means of reparation and atonement. As a result, the P text eliminates all references to other means of interacting with the divine such as dreams and angels. Components reflecting an overall design as an alternative to JE are identifiable in virtually every P story. The differences between the P versions and the JE versions of stories can all be explained in terms of promoting the overall interests and agenda of the Priestly author. For example, in J Noah takes seven pairs of clean animals on the ark (Gen 7:2,3) while in P he takes only one pair (Gen 6:19; 7:8, 9, 15), because in J Noah offers a sacrifice at the end and therefore needs more than one pair of the clean animals to avoid eliminating a species. In P, however, no sacrifices are depicted prior to Aaron, and therefore Noah does not need extra animals. Similarly, we can explain P's addition of Joshua alongside Caleb in the spies story (Num 14:6-9, 38). In JE, Joshua's merit as Moses' successor is established by his disassociation from the golden calf incident (Exodus 32-33). P omits the golden calf incident because it denigrates Aaron. Thus P needed a different way of demonstrating Joshua's legitimacy as successor to Moses.

If we allow that each of J, E, and P were each originally independent sources and that P was composed as a version of Israel's early history alternative to the redacted JE, then it is important to read each version on its own to determine each author's worldview, and in particular their attitudes toward magic. As W. Propp notes, if P is to be regarded as a "rival and alternative recension to the redacted JE," then "we must believe that the original P was basically internally consistent," and "one must read P without the intervening matter from JE to obtain a sense of its story line."[188] By doing so, interesting contrasts between the different authors' portrayals of magic emerge.

---

[187] See the arguments put forth by S. Mowinckel in *Erwagungen zur Pentateuch Quellenfrage* (Trondheim: Universitetsforlaget, 1964); R. E. Friedman in *The Exile and Biblical Narrative* (HSM 22; Chico: Scholars Press, 1981); and D. M. Carr, *Reading the Fractures of Genesis: Historical and Literary Approaches* (Lousville: Westminster John Knox Press: 1996).

[188] "The Rod of Aaron and the Sin of Moses," *JBL* 107/1 (1988) pp. 19-26.

In Chapter Two, we determined that the reason for prohibiting magic and divination in the Holiness Code was to restrict access to Yahweh to priests. Prophets are not even mentioned as legitimate communicators with the divine in the Holiness Code, or anywhere in the Priestly text. In fact, the word prophet appears only once in P, and it is in connection with Aaron, who is to be Moses' "prophet." In this context, the word is stripped of its supernatural connotation, indicating only that Aaron is to be Moses' "spokesperson."[189] In P, God does not communicate with prophets but with priests. According to P's narrative, Moses creates and inaugurates the priesthood as a successor institution to his own office as communicator between Yahweh and Israel.[190] Because he was dealing with well-known persons and stories, the author of P had to include details of Moses' supernatural abilities, but he was careful to demonstrate that they are unique to Moses (unlike D, for example, who states in Deut 18:18 that a prophet like Moses will arise in the future) and usually enacted by Aaron, the priest. In fact, the author of P is careful never to attribute any power to Moses himself, framing each magical event to demonstrate explicitly that Yahweh instructs Moses in every aspect of the execution of a magical act. The purpose is to show that Moses is merely a vessel channeling the power of Yahweh. He wields no magic in his own right, and when he attempts to do so in P's version of drawing water from a rock (Numbers 20:9-11), he is punished for it.[191]

This also accounts for the differences in the consequences for Korah, Dathan, and Abiram in Numbers 16. The stories of J and P are intertwined in this episode,[192] which describes a rebellion against Moses and Aaron. For P,

---

[189] W. H. C. Propp, *Exodus 1-18*, (New York: Doubleday, 2000) p. 282, remarks: "Exod 7:1 excellently illustrates P's ambivalence toward Moses and toward prophets in general. On the one hand, Moses is Aaron's superior, a quasi-deity. Yet he is unfit to address Pharaoh. Aaron the priest-to-be must serve as prophetic intermediary, delivering Yahweh's oracle against a foreign nation to its hostile ruler and performing wonders with his staff." Propp notes that this could be read as P polemicizing against prophets, "claiming that Aaronic priests are superior intermediaries."

[190] W. Propp, private communication. See also *Exodus 1-18*, pp. 284-86.

[191] Although the majority of modern commentators view this text as the result of the amalgamation of several sources, more convincing evidence for exclusively Priestly authorship is detailed in Propp, *Exodus 1-18*, especially p. 21; M. Margaliot, "Het(') mose(h) we'aharon beme meriba," *Beth Mikra* 19 (1974), pp. 374-400; P. J. Budd, *Numbers*, (Waco: Word, 1984); F. Kohata, "Die priesterschriftlich Uberlieferungsgeschichte von Numeri XX 1-13," *Annual of the Japanese Biblical Institute* 3 (1977) pp. 3-34; and G. W. Coats, *Rebellion in the Wilderness* (Nashville: Abingdon, 1968, pp. 71-82). Propp suggests that "the Priestly writer revised the Massah-Meribah account in order to explain the deaths of Moses and Aaron and to impute sin to the former" (p. 24).

[192] The P text includes vv 1a, 2b-11, 15-24, 26-27a, 32b, and 35. The remaining verses (1b-2a, 12-14, 25, 27b-32a, 33-34) constitute the J version.

Korah is the ring-leader, while in the J version Dathan and Abiram challenge Moses' authority. In each, a showdown between Moses and the rebels is required to settle the issue, but what is at stake, as well as the end results and the way in which they are enacted, are noticeably different. In the P text, Korah and other Levites seek more than Temple service; they challenge Moses and Aaron for the priesthood itself. In this story, P demonstrates that only Aaron and his descendants can serve as priests. Moses instructs Korah and his followers to test their ability to serve Yahweh as priests by having them offer incense, a privilege only of priests, alongside Aaron. Moses tells the rebels that God will indicate which group he considers holy and worthy of making such priestly offerings, but he does not specify how God will do this; that seems to be for Yahweh to decide. When they make their offering, God demonstrates his election of Aaron over all other Levites by sending fire to consume Korah and his followers. The incineration comes directly from God, and its purpose is explicit: no one other than descendants of Aaron has the right to act as a priest in Israel.[193]

In the J version, however, the issue is Moses' authority as Yahweh's representative and rightful leader of the people. Moses responds to the challengers by demonstrating his authority with a magical act. In vv 28–30, he calls in the name of Yahweh for the ground to open up and swallow the dissenters, so that "you will know that Yahweh sent me to do all these things." No sooner does Moses finish speaking than the ground opens and swallows Dathan, Abiram, and their families, bringing them alive to the netherworld of Sheol. The differences between this and the P version are striking: Moses dictates the nature of the magic far more explicitly in J, while Yahweh silently complies. The expressed purpose of Moses' actions is to support Moses' claim to be Yahweh's representative, and, as such, Moses has the power and authority to wield magic.

Other J texts support this view. The author of J seems to have even fewer restrictions on human ability to perform magic than E's writer does. J and E share common traditions about the magical and divinatory abilities of some legendary figures in Israel's history. For example, both have stories about Balaam's magical abilities in Numbers 22–24.[194] P mentions Balaam in Num 31:8, 16 only in connection with the apostasy at Peor and to note that he was killed in

---

[193] This purpose is reiterated in the commission of commemorative plating for the altar constructed out of the rebels' fire-holders, "a commemoration for the children of Israel in order that no outsider, one who is not from Aaron's seed, will come forward to burn incense before Yahweh, so he will not be like Korah and like his congregation, as Yahweh spoke to him by Moses' hand" (Num 17:5).

[194] For the division of Numbers 22-24 between the J and E sources, see: J. A. Hackett, "Some Observations on the Balaam Tradition at Deir ʿAllā," *BA* 49 (1986), pp. 216–22; W. Gross, *Bileam: Literar- und formkritische Untersuchung der Prosa in Num 22–24,* (Munich, 1974); S. Mowinckel, "Der Ursprung der Bileamsage," *ZAW* 48 (1930), pp. 233–71; and R. R. Wilson, *Prophecy and Society in Ancient Israel* (Philadelphia: Fortress Press, 1980).

battle against Israel. Also in J, Joshua causes the sun to stop its motion for an entire day. [195] The magnitude of this magical act was so remarkable that the author noted that: "There was nothing like that day, before it and after it, regarding Yahweh's listening to a man's voice" (v 14). But not all miracles are instigated by humans. For instance, when the walls of Jericho are magically brought down in Joshua 6, J notes that Joshua is following explicit instructions from Yahweh. Likewise when the Israelites cross the Jordan in Joshua 3. In all of these incidents, J is never concerned with labeling Joshua as a "prophet." And the fact that Joshua was not even from the tribe of Levi, let alone a priest, does not bother the author of J in the least. For J, the status of the person performing a magical act seems almost immaterial. The Priestly text, on the other hand, demonstrates Joshua's dependency on priestly mediation to communicate with Yahweh, an intercession that Moses himself had not needed.[196]

For P, no human ever really performs magic. The miraculous always directly involves Yahweh, who may make use of a human being to perform wonders, but no person ever wields supernatural abilities in his own right. And not even Moses or Aaron can *appear* to do so without dire consequences. This is not the case for the other biblical authors. The Elohist is also careful to demonstrate that Moses' power is granted to him from Yahweh, but he is more willing to allow that the power does reside in the person of Moses. The difference is subtle but important. Unlike P, for E Moses was a prophet. He was not a human vessel through which Yahweh's power could be demonstrated, but rather he was Yahweh's representative to the people. He carried messages from God, and in order to establish his legitimacy in their eyes he was given the ability to perform "signs." E makes this explicit at the burning bush, and the magical feats Yahweh gives him there convince the Israelites that Moses does represent Yahweh (Exod 4:30-31). In contrast, in the P text Moses does not perform wonders for the people, but rather Aaron does them for Pharaoh and his courtiers. By the third plague, the author of P has the Egyptian magicians recognizing that these

---

[195] Josh 10:12-13. We are adopting the perspective that J is part of a text that extends beyond the Torah, as a source for the Deuteronomistic History. See Friedman, *The Hidden Book in the Bible* (San Francisco: Harper, 1998); and E. Auerbach, *Mimesis* (Princeton: Princeton University Press, 1968), p. 12. Several other scholars have noted striking linguistic, literary, and thematic similarities between the two texts, although they have fallen short of ascribing them to the same hand: see especially R. Polzin, *Late Biblical Hebrew: Toward an Historical Typology of Biblical Hebrew Prose*, HSM (Atlanta: Scholar's Press, 1976); L. Boadt, *Reading the Old Testament: An Introduction* (New York: Paulist Press, 1984); J. Rosenberg, *King and Kin* (Bloomington, IN: Indiana University Press, 1986); Y. Zakovitch, "Assimilation in Biblical Narratives," in *Empirical Models for Biblical Criticism*, ed. J. Tigay (Philadelphia: University of Pennsylvania Press, 1985), pp. 185-92; and R. Clements, *Abraham and David* (London: SCM, 1967).

[196] See Num 27:15–23: Joshua's word must be confirmed by Eleazar the priest's *ûrîm* (v 21).

are not mere magic tricks, but something far more powerful: "this is the finger of God!" (Exodus 8:15).

This subtle difference is carried through the portrayals of the plagues in both E and P. P's plagues demonstrate the enormous power of Yahweh, enacted through his human agents Moses and Aaron, beyond anything the Egyptian magicians can wield. E's plagues also prove Yahweh's power, but Moses' function is different. He is to *carry messages* warning Pharaoh of the consequences for his refusal to let the Israelites go free, consequences that their God will produce if the prophet's words are not heeded. In both cases, the power is God's, but for E Moses acts as the deity's messenger: first he brings words of warning and then he brings about the plagues on God's behalf.

In P, Moses and Aaron simply carry out a series of instructions given by Yahweh. Almost every P plague follows the same pattern: "And Yahweh said to Moses, "Say to Aaron, 'Take your staff and reach out … and there will be blood/frogs/lice in all the land of Egypt.'" And they did so, and Aaron reached out his hand … and there was blood/frogs/lice in all the land of Egypt."[197] E's plague accounts also follow a pattern of instructions given by Yahweh and carried out by Moses. However, they are directions to Moses first to *prophesy* to Pharaoh regarding the consequences of ignoring Yahweh's request to let his people go. In each case, Moses is told to go to Pharaoh and say some variation of the following: "Thus says Yahweh: 'Let my people go. And if you refuse, I will bring blood/frogs/beasts/livestock disease/hail/locusts (tomorrow[198])." … And Moses/they/Yahweh did so…."[199]

God is credited with bringing the plagues in both P and E. The role of Moses and Aaron is less clear. In P it seems that they are vessels for the expression of Yahweh's power, carrying out instructions from God that result in plagues. In E, too, Moses carries out Yahweh's directions, but as a prophet does: first delivering a warning, and then effecting the consequences on Yahweh's behalf. The difference thus hinges on the question of who can legitimately perform magic. For P, only priests can communicate with the divine; prophecy as an institution does not exist. As a priest, Aaron speaks to Pharaoh and works

---

[197] For this pattern in P's version of the plagues, see Exodus 7:19f, 8:1f, 8:12f. Propp (*Exodus 1-18*) notes that the changing commands to Aaron (7:9, 7:19, 8:1, 8:12) are a matter of "variety for variety's sake" (p. 311). P deviates from the pattern somewhat in 9:8, when Yahweh speaks to both Moses and Aaron, and Moses is commanded to throw the soot to produce the plague of boils (see Propp's *Exodus 1-18*, pp. 331-32 for possible reasons for this deviation). And in 12:12 Yahweh tells Moses and Aaron that he himself will go through the land of Egypt bringing death to the Egyptians' firstborn.

[198] Exodus 8:19, 9:5, 9:18.

[199] See Exodus 7:14f, 7:26f, 8:16f, 9:1f, 9:13f, and 10:1f. For the attribution of all of these plagues to the single E source, see Propp's thorough argument in *Exodus 1-18*, pp. 310-17.

wonders; in P, the only divine mediators are the Aaronid priests. On the other hand, emphasis on prophecy is a recurrent theme in the E text of the Torah. In E, prophets have the ability to communicate with God, the authority to speak on his behalf, and can demonstrate this with acts of power, as evidenced from Moses' commission at the burning bush and through the rest of his career.

In P, Moses is never responsible for acts of power in his own right; as we have seen, Yahweh always gives detailed instructions to him, and then Moses follows the instructions to the letter. In fact, all of the magic that is enacted by Moses in the Priestly text has a parallel story in JE; P does not ever credit magic to Moses unless there is a precedent text with which an Israelite audience would have been familiar, and its omission in P's version would have been noticeable. P had to reconcile a tradition of Moses as miracle-worker with the priestly laws that forbid magic by anyone other than a priest and that ignore the existence of prophets almost entirely. P does so by having Aaron (the future high priest) perform the majority of the magical feats, and by ensuring that there is no question of the humans possessing any power of their own. E, on the other hand, is less restricted: in fact, it is E who identifies the power wielded by prophets as often necessary to prove their legitimacy to the people. In doing so, E sets the stage for literary portrayals of future prophets able to wield magical powers in their own right.

Elijah and Elisha

Both B. Long[200] and T. Overholt[201] suggest that, like E's portrayal of Moses, the magical activities of Elijah and Elisha "served to demonstrate their legitimacy and reinforce their claims of authority."[202] It is important to note, however, that there are subtle differences between the magic wielded by Elijah and Elisha on one hand, and that of Moses and Aaron on the other. Many of the magical activities of Elijah and especially Elisha are not attributed to God at all. Even when these men call on God for help they initiate each miracle, often take credit for their powers, and never need explicit instructions from Yahweh on the correct performance of a magical act.[203]

---

[200] B. Long, "The Social Setting for Prophetic Miracle Stories," *Semeia* 3 (1975): pp. 46-59.

[201] T. Overholt, *Channels of Prophecy* (Minneapolis: Fortress Press, 1989), especially pp. 86-111.

[202] Overholt, p. 111.

[203] In *The Disappearance of God* (New York: Little, Brown and Co., 1995), R. E. Friedman demonstrates that this is part of a gradual shift of the locus of control, from God to humanity.

This is evident from the first time we meet Elijah in the text. He tells Ahab: "As Yahweh God of Israel lives, before whom I have stood, there will not be in these years dew or rain *except by my word*" (1 Kgs 17:1). In this opening statement, Elijah establishes that he is a prophet of Yahweh but swears in the name of Yahweh that the drought will not end until he *himself* declares it over. Elijah acknowledges the hand of Yahweh in many of his magical actions, but in the narrative itself, there is no indication that he is acting on Yahweh's *instructions*, only on His behalf. In this first example, we are not told that Elijah is acting according to God's word, and in fact Elijah gets away with exactly the behavior for which Moses is so severely punished in Numbers 20 – he claims credit for the drought.

A similar pattern is apparent in Elijah's subsequent miracles. Many are of a personal rather than public nature, and all are initiated at Elijah's own decision, although Yahweh is usually acknowledged as his source of power. When he produces endless flour and oil for a poor widow in 1 Kgs 17:13-16, he says "thus says Yahweh God of Israel: the jar of flour will not cease, and the jug of oil will not lack, until the day that Yahweh gives rain upon the face of the earth." When he later resurrects the widow's son (1 Kgs 17:20-22) it is also at his own initiative, but the deed is only accomplished when Elijah prays to Yahweh on the boy's behalf. Elijah also prays during the public contest between Yahweh and Baal at Mt. Carmel that he sets up, and when he does, Yahweh brings lightning and rain (1 Kgs 18:30-38). The purpose of the contest is to demonstrate Yahweh's power to end the drought, not Elijah's, but the fact that Elijah is credited with this success is demonstrated by Jezebel's murderous fury at him to the extent that he has to flee the country.

The use of magic to support Elijah's claim to be a prophet of Yahweh is explicit in 2 Kgs 1:9-14. Ahaziah king of Samaria sends several army troops to bring Elijah into custody. When the first two approach and request that he descend from his mountain and accompany them, Elijah answers each captain of fifty in the same way: "If I am a man of God, let fire come down from the heavens and consume you and your fifty men." And no sooner does he call for it than "fire from God descended from the heavens and consumed him and his fifty men." Elijah himself initiates and dictates the nature of the magic, and God immediately complies; and it is all performed in the interest of demonstrating Elijah's status as a "man of God" and his authority to speak on Yahweh's behalf. Similarly, the earlier miracles that Elijah performs for the widow and her son provoke the following reaction from the woman: "Now [by] this I know that you are a man of God and the word of Yahweh in your mouth is true" (1 Kgs 17:24).

The final act of magic performed by Elijah is not only initiated by him but, unlike the others, is accompanied neither by prayer to Yahweh nor by invoking

---

With respect to the position of Elijah and Elisha in this transfer of power, see especially pp. 51-59.

His name as the author of the act. In 2 Kgs 2:8 Elijah crosses the Jordan by striking it with his cloak and causing the water to divide. This is Elijah's last, and then Elisha's first, act of magic. Notably, when Elisha tries it the first time, it does not work. Then he asks, "Where is Yahweh, the God of Elijah?" as he strikes the river a second time – and the waters part for him then (2 Kgs 2:14). Likewise, when Elisha is called on to perform his second act of magic, purifying polluted water, he does so in Yahweh's name, giving Yahweh full credit, and is successful: "thus says Yahweh, I have healed these waters..." (2 Kgs 2:21). Even when he next uses magic, and this time for his own dubious ends, invoking the name of Yahweh seems to bring success: in 2 Kgs 2:24, when he curses in the name of Yahweh the children who taunt him, they are immediately mauled by two bears.

There are many more magical acts attributed to Elisha in the Bible than to Elijah, and a greater percentage of Elisha's magic occurs without any mention of Yahweh. Like Elijah, Elisha multiplies food with the statement, "thus says Yahweh" (4:42-44), but when he causes oil to proliferate for a widow (2 Kgs 4:1-7), he does so without invoking God or attributing success to Him. He also de-toxifies stew (2 Kgs 4:38-41), makes an ax-head float (6:6-7), gives "leprosy" to his servant Gehazi (5:25-27), and helps Joash magically divine the number of victories he will have over Syria (13:17-19), all without even mentioning Yahweh. Some of his magical acts do require prayer, however, such as his replication of Elijah's feat of resurrecting a boy (4:31-37), or when he causes the Aramaean army to hallucinate and withdraw (6:8-23).

As with E's Moses, and Elijah before him, Elisha's magic seems to be a function of his status as a prophet and serves to demonstrate his authority as a messenger of Yahweh as well as provide testimony to the power of Israel's God. The healing of Naaman's "leprosy" is cast in this light when Elisha tells the king of Israel that he should send Naaman to Elisha, "that he will know that there is a prophet in Israel" (5:8). Interestingly, Naaman expects far more ceremony, including the invocation of the Israelite God (5:11), to accompany Elisha's magical act than Elisha provides. Elisha does not call on Yahweh at all, simply advising Naaman via a servant to bathe in the Jordan seven times. Regardless of the lack of involvement of Yahweh in the magical healing, however, when it works the magic serves a particular function. Naaman exclaims, "Now I know that there is no god on all the earth but in Israel" (5:15). The gift he offers in recompense, however, is to Elisha, not to Yahweh.

Thus when prophets wield magic in both E and the Elijah-Elisha cycles, their acts accomplish the dual purposes of testifying to the power of Yahweh and demonstrating the authority of His messenger. The fundamental difference between the majority of portrayals of Moses' magic and those of Elijah and Elisha lie in who initiates and who is credited with the efficacy of the act. In P, neither Moses nor Aaron performs magic without step-by-step guidance from Yahweh, and when Moses' statement to the Israelites appears to ascribe the power to draw

water from the rock to himself and Aaron rather than to Yahweh, he has committed his most serious sin.[204]   In contrast, Elijah and especially Elisha suffer no
consequences for both explicitly and implicitly taking credit for the magic they
perform. In fact, there seems to be a fundamental difference between the ways
in which their magic is understood to operate. In both E and P, the authors often
go to great lengths to demonstrate that the power behind Moses' acts belongs to
Yahweh. Elijah and Elisha, however, call their own miracles, only sometimes
having to ask Yahweh for help in their accomplishment. Furthermore, particularly in the case of Elisha, the magic seems to reside not in Yahweh but rather in
the person of the prophet. This is nowhere more apparent than in 2 Kgs 13:21,
when a dead man is resurrected after coming into contact with Elisha's bones in
his grave. Yahweh is not mentioned, and no one actually performs any magic.
Rather the corpse of the dead prophet itself retains a miraculous quality with the
power of resurrection on contact.

   Scholars often note the striking parallels between the accounts of Moses in
Exodus and the events in Elijah's career.[205]   The majority conclude that these
similarities occur because the authors of E and of the Northern source for the
Deuteronomistic History arise from the same circle of prophets.[206]   In the case of
Elijah, the stories about him purposely draw on the legends of the greatest
prophet (for E), Moses: "The cumulative impact of these extensive Mosaic allu-
sions is to present Elijah as a Moses *redivivus*."[207]   The Northern traditions from
which the stories of Elijah and Elisha are drawn strongly match E's emphasis on
the importance of prophets as well as their magical abilities. Many scholars have
also noted in general the similar sympathies and emphases of the E text and the
Northern sources of the Deuteronomistic History. P. K. McCarter postulates a
pre-Deuteronomic level of redaction from a prophetic perspective in this material. He suggests that the "prophetic historian" collected the oldest sources un-

---

[204] When Moses says "shall *we* draw water from this rock?" it is not even clear that he does
not mean "God and I" rather than "Aaron and I." This understanding by God can only be
inferred from the fact that Aaron is also punished, presumably because it is a conclusion that
the Israelites might have drawn from Moses' statement. In fact, when instructing Moses,
God says "You shall bring water from the rock." The sin seems to have been committed
when Moses claimed the initiative for his actions because he failed to sanctify Yahweh *to his
Israelite audience*. Thus, even if Moses had intended "God and I" by his "we," in light of the
careful way in which P elsewhere attributes Moses' miracles to God's power, it would seem
that according to the logic of the overall narrative, this would have been enough cause for the
punishment that Moses receives.

[205] For example, compare the events of 1 Kings 18:31-40 with Exodus 24:2-6 and 32:12-28.

[206] See J. T. Walsh, *1 Kings* (Minneapolis: Liturgical Press, 1996).

[207] J. T. Walsh, "Elijah," *The Anchor Bible Dictionary* (New York: Doubleday, 1992).

derlying the books of Samuel, and that this prophetic redaction may have served as a major source for Dtr1's account of the monarchy.[208]

Despite the similar empowerment of prophets in E and the Northern source, we have also seen important differences between them with respect to the portrayals of Elijah and Elisha's magic and that with which Moses is credited. Like P, E is careful to demonstrate that the source of Moses' power is Yahweh, and in almost every case Moses' magic is a result of carrying out explicit instructions that Yahweh gives him. The author of the Northern source is far less concerned with demonstrating Yahweh's tutelage behind every magical action of his prophets. Secondly, for E Moses' powers have been granted to him for the sole purpose of effectively carrying out his prophetic mission to the Israelites. In the cases of Elijah and Elisha, this is only really true of the contest at Mt. Carmel that Elijah stages between Baal and his prophets, and Yahweh. The magical events in the story in 1 Kings 18 are designed to prove to the public that Yahweh is the one true God. The remainder of Elijah's and Elisha's feats are private displays of their power as Yahweh's representatives. The E stories of Moses contain no such personal miracles. For E, Moses' prophetic mission is to the people of Israel as a whole.[209]

While P emphasizes the power of priests to the exclusion of any other mediator between God and humanity, the focus in E is the power of prophets. But it is not a power taken lightly by the author; like P, the author of E is reluctant to show humans wielding such power at will. And like P, though to a lesser extent, the author of E is careful to demonstrate Yahweh's hand behind Moses' actions. The Northern Source in this respect is quite dissimilar from the E source. The prophets Elijah and Elisha are much more powerful in their own right than E allows Moses to be. In this respect, they are closer to J's portrayal of magicians; J seems less concerned than E about showing humans in control of magic, as we saw in Numbers 16 and Joshua 10, for example. The difference between J and the Northern Source is the emphasis in the Northern Source on prophets, which J lacks.

Thus our findings regarding the respective attitudes toward magic among the different authors of the sources of the Tetrateuch confirm and reinforce much of the source critical scholarship that has been concerned with who these authors were and out of which circles they arose.[210] That the author of P is a priest with

---

[208] See his *I Samuel* and *II Samuel* (Anchor Bible, New York: Doubleday, 1980 and 1984).

[209] For the distinction between public and private miracles and the gradual transition in biblical narrative from the former to the latter, and then to the complete cessation of miracles, see Friedman, *The Disappearance of God*, pp. 7-90.

[210] See especially F. M. Cross, *Canaanite Myth and Hebrew Epic* (Cambridge: Harvard, 1973); and R. E. Friedman, *Who Wrote the Bible?* (New York: Simon and Schuster, Summit, 1987).

vested interest in the Aaronid priesthood is readily apparent. E's attribution of power to prophets yet careful portrayal of Yahweh's hand behind their actions in a manner similar to P demonstrates this author's balance between prophetic interests and those of non-Aaronid priests. The Shilonite circle around the figure of Samuel provides a likely setting for such an attitude toward magic.[211] The J stories about magic do not reflect the interests of either priests or prophets. And the Northern Source responsible for the Elijah and Elisha stories promotes the idea of prophets of Yahweh as having super-human powers that they can wield at will for their own ends, a view that prophetic circles would have a definite interest in promoting.

Outside the Tetrateuch, not all biblical prophets are credited with magical powers. In fact, with one exception, the writing prophets do not possess supernatural abilities. Their messages are delivered through the power of their words, their long, divinely-inspired speeches. Elijah and Elisha rarely deliver prophetic speeches, and when they do they are not of the same genre as the writing prophets' poetic warnings and criticisms. Their message, concerning the supreme power of Yahweh and his control over all things in nature, is rather delivered through their magical actions, making them different kinds of prophets from the writing prophets in the Hebrew Bible.

Isaiah

The one exception to our observations about the writing prophets occurs in a story about the prophet Isaiah. When King Hezekiah is deathly ill, Isaiah prophesies that he will not die, and in fact he will heal so quickly that in three days' time Hezekiah will enter the Temple. In 2 Kgs 20:9-10, Hezekiah asks Isaiah for a sign that his prophecy will come to pass, and Isaiah requests that Hezekiah choose whether the shadow on the steps[212] should advance or retreat. Hezekiah asks that the shadow magically retreat; Isaiah calls on Yahweh, and the shadow retreats. In the parallel version recounted in Isa 38:7-8, Hezekiah neither requests a sign nor determines its content. Rather, Isaiah volunteers both, saying "And this will be a sign for you from Yahweh, that Yahweh will do the thing of which he spoke. Here I am causing to return the shadow of the steps...." According to the version in the book of Isaiah, the sign is from Yahweh, acting through the agency of his prophet Isaiah. In the narrative of 2 Kings, however, Isaiah and Hezekiah determine the nature of the sign, and Isaiah calls on Yahweh for its execution.

---

[211] See Friedman, *Who Wrote the Bible?*

[212] Although often translated "sundial," 1QIsa[a] supports a reading of "steps" in this passage. See S. Iwry, "The Qumran Isaiah and the End of the Dial of Ahaz," *BASOR* 147 (1957), pp. 27-33; and R. E. Friedman, *The Disappearance of God*, p. 25.

There are several things worth noting about these two versions of the same story. In both, a sign seems to be a natural thing to ask or grant to demonstrate the legitimacy of a prophetic statement. As we have seen, many of the prophets in the Hebrew Bible make use of signs to underscore or lend authority to their prophecies. Most, however, are of a symbolic rather than a magical nature: Isaiah is the only writing prophet who is also credited with magical powers. But the text recounts the episode in the same casual way in which it tells of other, symbolic, prophetic signs. Secondly, in Isaiah 38 Yahweh pre-determines the sign, volunteers it to Hezekiah through the agency of Isaiah, and Isaiah executes it. In the context of 2 Kings, however, Hezekiah decides what the sign will be (within the limits Isaiah has set), and Isaiah calls on Yahweh to perform it. In a manner reminiscent of P's accounts of Moses and Aaron's magic, the emphasis in the account in the Book of Isaiah is on Isaiah's function as a vessel for God's messages and actions. Isaiah, like so many spokespeople for Yahweh in the Hebrew Bible, is portrayed as insisting that he is not responsible for the messages he delivers; they originate with God and merely operate through him. His ability to execute the magical sign only underscores that he is a true representative of Yahweh's message. On the other hand, for witnesses of prophetic actions, it must have been very difficult to distinguish between the actions of the prophet on his own behalf and those that were divinely inspired.

It might be instructive to view the narratives of Elijah's and Elisha's feats in the same light. Whether or not Yahweh is credited with initiating, controlling, determining, or having been invoked in recounting the magical actions of these prophets seems almost arbitrarily determined (in stark contrast to the careful way in which most of Moses' magic is demonstrated to derive directly from God. To the non-prophet outsider who witnessed or passed on the stories of Elijah and Elisha, it must have seemed as though they themselves controlled the magic.

Conclusions

Magical acts thus pervade the narrative of the Tetrateuch and in fact are portrayed as determining factors in Israelite history. Magic occurs at the foundation of the nation. It serves to establish Moses' authority as leader of the Israelites and also works to free them from slavery. Magic sustains the people in the wilderness, quenching their thirst and healing their snake-bites. And magic is necessary for their entry into the Promised Land under Joshua, both when the Jordan parts and when the Israelites conquer Canaanite territory such as Jericho. Magic continues during the establishment of the Israelite nation in its land as it serves to legitimize the position of prophets who speak and act on Yahweh's behalf.

The problem for some of the authors of this history was the question of who could perform magic. If *anyone* was entitled, then it detracted from both the authority of cult officials, i.e., the priests and prophets who mediated between Yahweh and His people, and also from the supreme power of Yahweh Himself. The divinatory ability of a necromancer was particularly dangerous, as we saw in 1 Samuel 28, because she could obtain powerful oracles when Yahweh Himself refused to give them. It is notable that out of the three authors of sources of the Tetrateuch whose work we have examined thus far, the one least concerned with the question of who can perform magic and divination is the only biblical author who is not a priest: J. Nor is J overly concerned with prophecy, a theme the author of E emphasizes continually. For J, the question of who can perform magic, and how, is simply a non-issue.

In the E text, the author ties the practice of magic to the notion of a "sign" by which a true prophet of Yahweh can be known. Thus for E, it is explicitly prophets or representatives of Yahweh who can both divine and wield magical powers, and this seems to be the inspiration for the author of the Deuteronomistic History's Northern source that details the feats of Elijah and Elisha.

The issue of magical ability is even more important to the author of P. For P, the only legitimate intercessors with Yahweh are the Aaronid priests; there are no prophets, other than Aaron. The author of the P narrative rewrote the history of the Israelite people from this perspective. Where he could not get around a received tradition of magic wielded by Moses, he carefully portrayed every act of magic originating with Yahweh and serving Yahweh's purposes. And then he recast the story of drawing water from a rock to demonstrate explicitly the severe punishment for a person – even Moses himself – who had the *hubris* to claim magical ability without attribution to Yahweh. P demonstrates Moses's unique position in Israelite history as the predecessor to the priesthood and also shows the passing of this torch as God's intermediary to Aaron. In P, there is no magic prior to the appearance of Moses. After Moses and Aaron, no non-priestly individual in P will perform magical acts either, and only priests will be able to act as God's intermediaries.

That is not to say that there is no more magic in P. The magic that priests wield is actually quite powerful, and fully legitimated in the cult. A magical conception lies at the heart of some of the most important priestly rituals that P describes in the Torah. We will examine some of these in the following chapter. Additionally, we will turn to the issue of the final source of the Torah, and how D and Dtr understand magic and incorporate it into Israelite history.

Chapter 4

Priestly Magic and the Magical Worldview

Priestly Magic

In Chapter Two we discussed priestly divinatory abilities in the context of the Holiness Code's sanctions against lay practitioners, which were designed to eliminate their competition. In the biblical narratives, priests are the only ones other than prophets or "men of God" who are described as performing magic and divination regularly.[213] Their magical abilities are manifest in two different forms: acts, and rituals.

Priestly acts of divination include the casting of lots (e.g. 1 Chronicles 24-26; Neh 10:35), the use of the ephod (1 Sam 23:9-13; 30:7-8), and the Urim and Thummim (Num 27:21; 1 Sam 14:41). In the P version of the plagues, it is Aaron (the future high priest) who is responsible for performing the majority of them with his rod (Exod 7:19f; 8:1f, 12f). The only other *act* of magic (as opposed to the rituals we shall discuss below) ascribed to priests occurs in a passage that is not part of the Priestly text, in the book of Joshua (3:7-17). In it, God tells Joshua to instruct the priests to carry the ark of Yahweh into the Jordan, which will then part so that the people can cross on dry land. The purpose is, as Joshua tells the Israelites: "By this you will know that a living God is among you" (3:10). From the story it seems that the ark is the key to the performance of this magical act. Only the priests are allowed to touch it,[214] so in a sense they are responsible for the magic. The perspective of the story, however, keeps the focus on Yahweh and Joshua, with the priests as silent collaborators bearing the ark according to their instructions.

This passage ends with Josh 4:14: "In that day Yahweh made Joshua great in the eyes of all of Israel, and they feared him as they had feared Moses all the days of his life." Thus, even though the priests carry the ark, the narrative emphasizes that this magical act, as in the E texts we discussed in Chapter Three, demonstrates "that a living God is among you" and designates Joshua as His legitimate representative.

Unlike the prophets discussed in Chapter Three, within the Bible the priests (other than Aaron) do not perform many acts of magic. Rather, they are responsible for the magic involved in priestly rituals. As we saw, in E it is the prophets who mediate between God and the people in the forms of divination

---

[213] Aside from the woman of En-Dor (see Chapter Two).

[214] The danger for laymen in touching the ark are made patently clear in 2 Sam 6:6-7, when the well-intentioned Uzzah is struck dead by God for grasping it.

and magic. In P, the priests are the intermediaries between the divine and human realms, and their magic is manifest almost exclusively through the power of rituals. The use of rituals that operate on magical premises demonstrates the existence of a magical worldview in ancient Israel: a perspective on the way things work that is not exclusively tied to empirical laws of cause and effect. This is a worldview that is shared throughout the ancient Near East, exemplified in widespread healing and fertility rituals, the use of execration, and the belief in the power of cursing. The Priestly text is replete with examples of rituals that effect results that have no physical, causal connection to the initiating actions of the participants. In fact, most biblical rituals that are generally classified as "religious" have an underlying magical premise, which is indicative of the difficulty of separating "religion" from "magic" in ancient Israel. Two priestly rituals particularly stand out in this regard: the "trial" of the suspected *sôṭāh* in Numbers 5, and the symbolic transference of Israel's sins to a scapegoat in Leviticus 16.[215] We shall examine Numbers 5 and Leviticus 16 in detail, and then the ritual of sacrifice in general, to demonstrate the ways in which Priestly religious ritual partakes of a magical worldview.

The *sôṭāh* Ritual

The only possible[216] case of trial by ordeal in the Hebrew Bible is that of the suspected *sôṭāh* in Numbers 5. If a woman's husband suspects her of having committed adultery but has no evidence or witnesses, he takes her to a priest who administers the *sôṭāh* ritual. In this ritual she must drink "*mê hammārîm hamĕ'ārĕrîm*": a mixture of holy water, dust from the floor of the Tabernacle, and ink from a written curse that is to take effect if she is guilty.

---

[215] There are other priestly rituals that also fall into this category of rites with magical premises. For example, the purification rite for scale disease (Leviticus 14) and the rite involving a broken-necked heifer (Deuteronomy 21) share direct parallels with the scapegoat ritual that will be discussed below (for the similarly operant concepts among these rituals, see especially J. Milgrom, *Leviticus 1-16*, Anchor Bible Commentary Series, [New York: Doubleday, 1991], pp. 1045 and 1082).

[216] K. Van der Toorn ("Ordeal," *The Anchor Bible Dictionary*) argues that there are several drinking ordeals described in the Bible, including the texts of Exod 15:22–26 and Exodus 32:20, and all of the references to the "cup of wrath" throughout the Prophets and Psalms (Isa 51:17–23; Jer 25:15–29; 49:12; 51:7, 39; Ezek 23:31–34; Obad 16; Hab 2:15–16; Zech 12:2; Pss 60:5; 75:9; Lam 4:21). He also suggests that the case of the suspected *sôṭāh* in Numbers 5 is not technically a "trial by ordeal" but rather describes the administration of a curse that is enacted only if the woman is guilty. He distinguishes among "oath," "curse," and "ordeal." However we choose to classify it, the magical premises of the *sôṭāh* ritual are unmistakable and are the same as those operative in other ancient Near Eastern trials by ordeal, oaths, and curses. See below.

The root of the word *mĕ'ărărîm* (*'rr*) indicates that the waters carry a curse that will be invoked if the woman is indeed guilty of adultery. The traditional translation of *mê hammārîm* in both the Targum and the Vulgate is "bitter waters." However, several scholars have argued that the addition of dust and ink to water is not likely to make the water "bitter"[217]: thus many alternative translations have been suggested. Noth posits that the bitter nature of the water is a symbolic one, the "bitterness of death,"[218] but this is doubtful as death is nowhere suggested in the passage. Driver links *mārîm* with *mārāh*, "to be rebellious" and translates the phrase as "waters of contention."[219] Sasson suggests relating *mārîm* to Ugaritic *mrr*, which parallels *brk* "to bless" in poetic usage.[220] This would make *mê hammārîm hamĕ'ărărîm* a *merismus* of "waters that bless" and "waters that curse," resulting in his translation "waters of judgment." Frymer-Kensky points out, however, that this interpretation does not explain the phrase *ûbā'û bāh hammāyim hamĕ'ărărîm lĕmārîm* of vv. 24 and 27.[221] She favors Brichto's translation, which he derives from the root *yrh*, "to teach": "waters of instruction, waters of revelation."[222] The term refers thus to the function of the waters in the trial, and the phrase in vv. 18, 19 and 24 should therefore be translated "the 'spell-effecting' revelation-waters." This translation best reflects the intended effects of the potion in the ritual but requires a derivation not otherwise attested.

The basis for these scholars' searches for an alternative to the root *mrr* is the assumption that dust and ink would not embitter holy water. However, although these explanations all have merit, perhaps the simplest translation is to be preferred: contrary to the statements of Driver and others, water can indeed be made bitter by the addition of ink, particularly if it was manufactured from soot.[223] The interpreta-

---

[217] G. R. Driver ("Two problems in the Old Testament examined in the light of Assyriology," *Syria* 33 [1956]) was the first to note this and attempt a different derivation for the term *mārîm*. He has been followed by a variety of other scholars, including T. Frymer-Kensky ("The Strange Case of the Suspected *sôṭāh* [Numbers v 11-31]," *VT* 34 [1984], pp. 11-26), J. Sasson ("Numbers 5 and the Waters of Judgment," *Biblische Zeitschrift* 16 [1972], pp. 249-51), and H. C. Brichto ("The Case of the *sôṭāh* and a Reconsideration of Biblical Law," *HUCA* 46 [1975], pp. 55-70).

[218] *Numbers: a commentary.* Trans. James D. Martin (Philadelphia: Westminster Press, 1968).

[219] G. R. Driver, "Two problems," p. 73.

[220] J. Sasson, "Numbers 5 and the Waters of Judgment."

[221] Frymer-Kensky, "The Strange Case of the Suspected *sôṭāh*."

[222] Brichto, "The Case of the *sôṭāh* and a Reconsideration of Biblical Law."

[223] The rabbis indicate that the ink mixture was manufactured out of a compound of soot, *gum arabica*, and water (*Sôṭāh* 2.4).

tion in the Targum and the Vulgate of *mê hammārîm hamē'ărărîm* as "bitter cursing waters" accords with the most obvious and recurrent use of the word *mārîm* in the Hebrew Bible, and makes perfect sense without imputing any other etymological derivations for the root.

More important than the taste of the potion is the intended effect of drinking "cursing waters." If the woman is innocent, the curse has no effect. If, however, "her womb[224] swells and her thigh sags" (v. 22), it is determined that she has committed adultery. In other words, if the woman is guilty, the curse carried by the waters will be enacted in her body.

The nature of the exact effects of swelling womb and sagging thigh is difficult to determine. Josephus suggested that the description fits the symptoms of edema.[225] Driver interprets this passage as indicating the occurrence of a miscarriage.[226] For Brichto, the punishment of the adulteress is sterility.[227] J. Milgrom similarly claims that this is a punishment designed to fit the crime: "the adulteress who acquiesced to receive forbidden seed is doomed to sterility for the rest of her life."[228] On the basis of an Akkadian root *ṣabû/ṣapû*, "to soak, flood," Frymer-Kensky also posits sterility as the ultimate result of the curse.[229] Translating *wĕṣābĕtâ biṭnāh* as "and her belly floods" rather than "and her belly swells," she argues that this refers to the punishment of the guilty adulteress in the form of a prolapsed uterus and subsequent infertility. In contrast, R. E. Friedman suggests that if a woman's womb is swelling and her thigh is sagging, it would seem rather that she is pregnant, and thus "The purpose of drinking the mixture is not to prove her guilt but to bring about the *curse* through her pregnancy."[230] Friedman argues that the ritual is meant for a woman who "has not slept with her husband recently, and that is why her pregnancy is proof of adultery."

---

[224] The Hebrew word *beṭen* is usually translated "belly," but R. E. Friedman, *Commentary on the Torah* (San Francisco: Harper, 2001), p. 440, points out that in each of its ten occurrences in the Torah the word literally means "womb."

[225] Josephus, *Antiquities* III:vi:6.

[226] Driver, "Two problems."

[227] Brichto, "The Case of the *śôṭāh* and a Reconsideration of Biblical Law."

[228] J. Milgrom, "The Case of the Suspected Adulteress, Numbers 5.11-31: Redaction and Meaning," in *The Creation of Sacred Literature*, ed. R. E. Friedman (Berkeley: University of California Press, 1981), pp. 69-75. See also Milgrom's *Numbers*, The JPS Torah Commentary (Philadelphia: Jewish Publication Society, 1990), p. 349.

[229] "The Strange Case of the Suspected *śôṭāh*."

[230] *Commentary*, p. 438.

Regardless of the nature of the physical enactment of the curse in the woman's body, the connection between the drinking of a bitter but otherwise harmless potion and its intended effects testifies to a belief in magic on the part of both the participants and the priestly administrators of the ritual. As A. Bach notes, "the magical (or divine) nature of the potion is that once inside the woman it discerns the purity or defilement of her body" and acts accordingly.[231] The combination of potion and priestly ritual magically effect a curse on the woman if she is indeed guilty of adultery.

The language that is used to describe the ritual likewise emphasizes the magical nature of this passage. The alliteration and wordplay heighten the mystery of the ritual with many repeated letter combinations and similar sounds from word to word. The phrase *mê hammārîm hamĕ'ărărîm* is the most obvious example of wordplay in the text, but Friedman[232] notes many others. For example, there are cases of reversals of root letters: *n`lm* of v 13 reverses *m`l* of v 27, in v 15 `*syrt* reverses *s`rym*, and in v 18 *pr`* reverses `*pr* of v 17. As Friedman points out, "each of these puns is linked to an aspect of this ceremony that is unique in some way: This is the only case in which *m`l* (to make a breach) is used for an offense against a human rather than God ..... It is the only time that *s`rym* (barley flour) is used for a grain offering. It is the only use of the `*pr* (dust) from the Tabernacle." The appearance of puns in a legal text is both unusual and unexpected: "they highlight the unusual aspect of this case, and they summon to mind associations with the realm of magic, in which the artistry of language and poetry figure in incantations and ceremonies."[233]

Form criticism also reveals a magical quality to this text that is absent from other biblical legal material. For example, Fishbane[234] argues that vv 29-30 form a topical resumption of vv 12-14 in a kind of subscript analogous to the resumptive repetitions characteristic of Akkadian prescriptive incantation-prayers and rituals against underworld demons[235] in the *Maqlû* series,[236] in the *Lamaštu* series,[237] and in the ritual tablets that accompany the Assyrian Dream Book.[238]

---

[231] A. Bach, "Good to the Last Drop: Viewing the *śôṭāh* (Numbers 5.11-31) as the Glass Half Empty and Wondering How to View It Half Full," in *Women in the Hebrew Bible, A Reader*, ed. Alice Bach (New York: Routledge, 1999), pp. 503-22.

[232] *Commentary* pp. 440-41.

[233] *Commentary*, pp. 440-41.

[234] M. Fishbane, "Accusations of Adultery: A Study of Law and Scribal Practice in Numbers 5:11-31," *HUCA* 45 (1974), pp. 25-45.

[235] E. Ebeling, *Tod und Leben nach den Vorstellungen der Babylonier* (Berlin, 1931), pp. 146-50.

[236] G. Meier, *Die Beschworungssammlung Maqlû, Archiv fur Orientforschung*, Beiheft 2 1937.

The *śôṭāh* ritual is designed to resolve a legal crisis. A serious crime might have been committed, but there is no evidence, and therefore no regular trial can be held. Adultery was a capital offense in ancient Israel, and thus a suspected but not proven *śôṭāh* presented a severe legal problem.[239] As in other ancient societies, such cases are presented before a divine trial by use of magical rituals.[240] The function of this procedure is not really to establish guilt in a legal sense for the purpose of conviction but rather to produce the curse if a woman is guilty. Notably, even if the physical conditions take effect, the woman is not executed; rather she "shall bear her crime" (5:31). Not only is the procedure fundamentally different from a legal one, but the punishment is left to God and not humanity to administer.

The underlying magical premises of the ritual are evident in the lack of a physical, causal connection between the prescribed actions (participating in the rituals and drinking the "bitter cursing water") and expected results (the curse either taking effect if the woman is indeed guilty, or not if she is innocent). The language,

---

[237] D. Myhrman, "Die Labartu-Texte," *ZA* 16 (1902), pp. 141-200.

[238] See A. L. Oppenheim "The Interpretation of Dreams" *Proceedings of the American Philosophical Society*, 46 (1955). Such repetitions and disjunctions in the text have also led a number of modern commentators to see the hands of two, sometimes three, separate authors and/or redactors in this pericope. See, for example, M. Noth's *Numbers, Old Testament Library* (London,1968) p. 49. Noth discerns an original magical ordeal with holy water underlying v 17, which was subsumed by the addition of a monotheistic oath in vv 19 and 21. Others who discern more than one hand in this text include B. Stade ("Beitrage zur Pentateuchkritik," sec. 3, "Die Eiferopferthora," *ZAW* 15 [1895], pp. 166-75), J. Gray (*Numbers* [Edinburgh: ICC, 1903], p. 49), and R. Rendtorff (*Die Gesetze in der Priestershcrift* [Gottingen, 1963], pp. 62-3). In contrast, more recent treatments of the subject emphasize the unity of the passage by analogy with other ancient Near Eastern materials (see for example the studies of M. Fishbane: "Accusations of Adultery," and *Studies in Biblical Magic: Origins, Uses and Transformations of Terminology and Literary Form* [diss: Brandeis] 1971), or by considerations of the internal format of the pericope (J. Milgrom, "The Case of the Suspected Adulteress"; H. C. Brichto, "The Case of the *śôṭāh*"; and T. Frymer-Kensky, "The Strange Case of the Suspected *śôṭāh*").

[239] Frymer-Kensky compares the case of the decapitated heifer described in Deut. 21:1-9: "The two crimes involved here – murder and adultery – are crucially dangerous to the fabric of Israelite society and are therefore punishable by death. In both circumstances – the discovery of a murdered body and the suspicions of a husband – it is impossible to "solve" the case by normal legal means … [thus] special quasi-legal procedures or rituals are prescribed to resolve the situation by religious means" (p. 11).

[240] T. Frymer-Kensky discusses trial by drinking-water ordeals described in Susa texts in her "The Judicial Ordeal in the Ancient Near East" (2 vols. Ph.D. Diss. Yale, 1977). J. M. Sasson ("Numbers 5 and the 'Waters of Judgment.'" *BZ* 16 (1972), pp. 249–51) finds evidence for a similar practice in Mari. Van der Toorn ("Ordeal") mentions Neo-Assyrian texts that show that a promissory oath (which he contrasts with the purgatory oath) could be accompanied by "drinking water from a *ṣarṣaru*-jar." He points out that the series *Šurpu* speaks of a "curse" *māmītu* incurred "by drinking water from a *ṣarṣaru*-jar" (III 62), and he suggests that "presumably, this water became harmful when the oaths were false."

parallels with water ordeals of other cultures, and the magical nature of oaths and curses combines with the concoction of a magic potion and ritual actions[241] to high-light the magical quality of this Priestly ritual.

The Scapegoat Ritual

Another ritual mediated by priests and with an explicitly magical set of prem-ises is the scapegoat ritual described in Leviticus 16. On *Yom Kippur*, in a rite de-signed to expunge sin from the Israelite people, the high priest was instructed to confess the sins of the people upon the head of a goat. This scapegoat was then sent into the wilderness, to "Azazel." Although the meaning, mechanism, and theo-logical implications of this rite are the subjects of debate, we will examine why its underlying magical premises are undeniable. The sins of the people are magically transferred to the head of a goat, which is banished to the uninhabited wilderness.

Banishment of evil to the wilderness was also practiced in ancient Mesopota-mia, where the word *ṣēru* (wilderness) is often used to designate the netherworld.[242] Hittite texts attest to a similar practice for the removal of impurity to uninhabited regions.[243] A related idea of evil dwelling in the wilderness is evident in Isa 13:21 and 34:14, in which Isaiah's prophecies that Babylon and Edom will become unin-habitable wastes include the notion that such demonic creatures as *tannîm* and *lîlît* will seek refuge there. The law of Leviticus 16 should be seen in this light, with some important qualifications to be discussed below. In general across the ancient Near East, "Elimination rites are … employed to drive the demons from human habitations and back to the wilderness, which is another way of saying that the de-mons are driven back to their point of origin, the underworld …. Thus, in Israel, the goat for Azazel bearing the sins of Israel, though it is bound for the wilderness, is in

---

[241] For example, the waving of the offering by the priest in vv 25f. Citing Hittite evidence, Fishbane (*Studies in Biblical Magic*) notes, "In general, waving is a magical act …. This ritual waving is frequent in investitive ceremonies and sacrifices in the Bible" (p. 255).

[242] Akkadian *hurbu (hurbatu)/namu (namutu)/kidi/tillanu/karmu* which are usually translated "ruins," "waste," or "desolation," can also refer to the netherworld; see K. Tallquist ("Sum- erisch-Akkadische Hymnen der Totenwelt," *Studia Orientalia* 4 [1934], pp. 17-22). Demons were believed to emerge from the netherworld through a hole in the ground; see Tawil ("Azazel the Prince of the Steppe: A Comparative Study," *ZAW* 92, pp. 43-59, especially pp. 48-50).

[243] See, for example, *The Ritual of Ambazzi* (*CTH* 391, II, lines 34-52; cf. *ANET* 348a), in which a mouse is employed to take away evil to "the high mountains, the deep valleys and the distant ways." Similarly, *The Ritual of Huwarlu* (*CTH* 398, II, lines 5-14) uses a dog to remove evil from the palace. Among the Hittites, there was a variety of ways in which impu-rity could be separated from the community; see D. P. Wright, *The Disposal of Impurity: Elimination Rites in the Bible and in Hittite and Mesopotamian Literature* (Atlanta: Scholars Press, 1987), pp. 45-60.

reality returning evil to its source, the netherworld." [244]   However, as Milgrom points out, the majority of ancient Near Eastern texts that demonstrate the existence of similar rituals among Israel's neighbors is designed toward achieving different goals. When animals (or sometimes people) are banished from the locus of civilization they are usually designated as either offerings to appease a god or an evil demon[245] or substitutes to divert evil from a person or a group onto another sacrificial being.[246] This is not the case in Leviticus 16.

Milgrom examines a number of ancient Near Eastern texts that share with the scapegoat ritual the idea of the *transference* of evil to the banished animal.[247] He argues, however, that even in these rituals the operant premises are essentially different from those in the scapegoat rite. In the majority of them evil is being removed from an individual, which Milgrom states is a fundamentally different concept from transferring and banishing the sins of an entire people.[248] Other important differences between the biblical rite and analogous ancient Near Eastern rituals are the fact that the goat for Azazel appears to be neither a sacrificial offering, as it carries impurities and would be unfit for such, nor a vicarious substitute for Israel, as no punishment of it is described in the text. Lev 16:22 simply states that "the goat will carry all their sins on it to an inaccessible land." As Wright notes, "There is no prayer to Azazel to make him act in a beneficent manner or to receive the goat as a substitute. The only active supernatural being in Lev 16 is Israel's God. The appearance of the motif of transfer alone, without appeasement and substitution, serves to underscore the centrality of God in this rite."[249]

Milgrom also emphasizes the depersonalization of Azazel in the biblical texts as compared with the living gods and demons to whom the Mesopotamians and

---

[244] J. Milgrom, *Leviticus 1–16*, Anchor Bible (New York: Doubleday, 1991), p. 1072.

[245] See, for example, *The Ritual of Uhhamuwa* (*CTH* 410; cf. *ANET* 347b) in which the god of an enemy is appeased by the offering of a decorated ram.

[246] This is exemplified in *The Ritual of Pulisa* (*CTH* 407) in which prisoners are offered to the enemy's god in the place of the king.

[247] From the Hittite corpus, Milgrom (*Leviticus 1–16*) refers to *The Ritual of Ambazzi* involving a mouse (*CTH* 391, II, lines 34-52; cf. *ANET* 348a) and to *The Ritual of Huwarlu*, in which evil is transferred to a dog (*CTH* 398, II, lines 5-14) (see n 31 above). See Milgrom (*Leviticus 1–16*), pp. 1075-76. The Mesopotamian texts that Milgrom compares to the ritual of Leviticus 16 include the rite of the Fifth Day of the *akitu*-Festival, as well as one from the *Utukke Limnuti* series (lines 115-38), and another from *Šurpu* (VII, 45-70). See Milgrom, pp. 1077-79.

[248] Milgrom (*Leviticus 1–16*) generalizes and emphasizes the differences between the biblical rite and those described in Mesopotamian and Hittite literature in a concise summary on p. 1079.

[249] Wright, *The Disposal of Impurity*.

Hittites directed their banished carriers of evil. Based on its use in post-biblical midrash as the name of a demon,[250] and parallel syntax in Leviticus 16 that designates one goat "for Yahweh" and the other "for Azazel," Milgrom concludes that Azazel is indeed the name of a divine being. However, in a fundamental difference between the scapegoat ritual and analogous Mesopotamian and Hittite rites, "Azazel himself is deprived of any active role: he neither receives the goat nor attacks it. Regardless of his origins – in pre-Israelite practice he surely was a true demon, perhaps a satyr (cf. Ibn Ezra on 16:8), who ruled in the wilderness – in the Priestly ritual he is no longer a personality but just a name, designating the place to which impurities and sins are banished."[251] For Milgrom, this transformation is inevitable in the Priestly monotheistic worldview.

Milgrom bases his understanding of the differences between magic and religion on the analysis of Y. Kaufmann,[252] who argues for a fundamental difference between pagan magico-mythological religion and Israelite monotheism. One aspect of this difference is an "absence in the Bible of the pagan conception of the demonic"[253]; according to Kaufmann, in ancient Israel, monotheism and a historical perspective replace mythology and magic to the extent that Israelite rituals that appear similar to pagan magical rites retain only a commemorative function.[254] Although Kaufmann admits the existence of "primitive" magical remnants among the Israelites, he argues that their meaning has been transformed to fit a non-mythological, non-magical, monotheistic consciousness. One of these surviving elements is the concept of ritual impurity.[255] In pagan religion, impurity is an expression of evil, demonic powers; Israel's purification rites never involved the demonic realm. Thus Israelite atonement is a pagan rite transmuted.[256]

B. Levine views the issues of magic and of ritual expiation in ancient Israel quite differently.[257] Unlike Kaufmann and Milgrom, Levine acknowledges the existence of magic in biblical rituals and argues that magic and religion worked

---

[250] See 3 Enoch 4:6 and Pirqe R. El. 46.

[251] Milgrom (*Leviticus 1-16*), p. 1021.

[252] Y. Kaufmann, *Toledot ha'emunah hayisra'elit* (Tel Aviv: Bialik Institute-Dvir), Vols. 1-7 (1937-1948). Translated and abridged from the Hebrew by M. Greenberg as *The Religion of Israel* (Chicago: University of Chicago Press, 1960). Citations and references herein refer to Greenberg's translation. See our discussion of Kaufmann's work in the Introduction.

[253] Kaufmann, *Toledot ha'emunah hayisra'elit*, p. 66.

[254] Kaufmann, *Toledot ha'emunah hayisra'elit*, p. 102.

[255] Kaufmann, *Toledot ha'emunah hayisra'elit*, pp.. 79-81, 102-04.

[256] Kaufmann, *Toledot ha'emunah hayisra'elit*, pp.. 114-15.

[257] See B. L. Levine, *In the Presence of the Lord* (Leiden: Brill, 1974), pp. 55-114.

together to combat evil and impurity. "To us it is clear that the distinctive objec-
tives of magical activity and those of the cult, proper, converged in pursuit of the
common end of eliminating destructive or demonic forces identified as the sources
of impurity, and viewed as the matrix of sinfulness and offense to the deity."[258] In
the scapegoat ritual, Levine sees an indirect battle between Yahweh and Azazel, in
which the high priest acts as God's intermediary. Levine argues that Azazel was not
a passive nonentity but rather ruled the wilderness, the source of impurity. In the
scapegoat ritual, the impurity resulting from sin is collected from the community
and returned to its source. However, Azazel would not have willingly received the
goat. Thus, when the high priest places his hands on the goat to confess over it, he
activates the power of Yahweh: "The priest infused the goat with potency by laying
his hands on it, transferring that potency which he had received [from the sanctu-
ary] to the scapegoat .... [This] implies that Yahweh indirectly combated `Azazel,
through the instrumentality of his priest, to whom he gave the power to propel the
goat into the wilderness. This means that `Azazel was conceived as an active force;
one to be countered by potent means."[259]

Against Levine, Milgrom argues that the function of confessing over the goat
is "judicial and not magical: to reduce the gravity of a nonexpiable wanton sin to an
inadvertency expiable by sacrifice .... Instead of fulfilling the magical objective of
infusing the scapegoat with the adytum's sacred power, the hand-leaning rite simply
transfers the sins of the people onto the goat, as expressly indicated by the text (v
21)."[260] Indeed, the text does state that the priest is simply transferring Israel's impurity to the goat: "Aaron shall lean both of his hands upon the head of the live goat
and confess over it all of the iniquities and transgressions of the Israelites, including
all of their sins, and *put them* on the head of the goat; and it shall be sent off to the
wilderness by a man in waiting. Thus the goat shall carry upon it all of their iniquities to an inaccessible land."[261] Levine's argument is largely unsupported by the
biblical text and seems to stem from his emphasis on Israel's similarity of thought
with Mesopotamia with respect to the existence of a powerful demonic realm that
poses a threat to Yahweh.

This dualism is absent from the biblical text. In Mesopotamian and Hittite
exorcisms, the divine beings to whom the impurities are delivered are understood as
active deities. For example, the *Šurpu* ritual shares a number of striking similarities
to the scapegoat ritual, with impurity-laden material sent for disposal to the wilderness, to the gods and beasts of the steppe.[262] "Yet it is in this very similarity that the

---

[258] Levine, *In the Presence of the Lord*, pp. 55-56.

[259] Levine, *In the Presence of the Lord*, p. 82.

[260] Milgrom, *Leviticus 1-16*, p. 1042.

[261] Leviticus 16:21-22 (emphasis mine).

[262] See *Šurpu* (VII, 45-70); Reiner 1958: pp. 36-38.

greatest contrast is found. The desert deities in Šurpu are very prominent and active. Ninkilim is called upon to act in transferring the evil to the vermin .... In contrast, Azazel does not act; he has no personality."[263] The ancient Near Eastern texts cited herein demonstrate many similarities in exorcistic function to the scapegoat ritual of Leviticus 16, which focuses on the transfer and removal of impurity from the people to a goat who will deliver it to the uninhabited wilderness. The hand-leaning is designed to remove the people's sins and place them on the goat.[264] However, the Mesopotamian and Hittite exorcistic rites seek to appease the gods, request their aid, or substitute a recipient for their anger. Conversely, as Milgrom and Kaufmann argue, the devitalization of Azazel in the scapegoat ritual shows that Leviticus 16 contains a transformation of an ancient rite of exorcism.

Just as similar ancient Near Eastern rituals designed to transfer evil from a person to an animal that is subsequently banished operate on the presumption of the magical efficacy of such actions, the scapegoat ritual can be presumed to work only if one adopts the worldview that such transference is possible. The prospect of a pronouncement or confession of sins acting as an agent of the *transference* of evil – whether from an individual *or* an entire nation – to another being, rests on the belief: (a) in the corruptive, physically harmful power of impurity deriving from moral iniquity; and (b) in the efficacy of spoken words and gestures to transfer or remove this impurity. In other words, one has to believe that these actions of confession over and banishment of the scapegoat both function to remove moral contamination without any physical causal connection between the action (confession and banishment), and the desired result (purity). The belief in the power of this ritual is thus a belief in the power of magic.

Sacrifice

From this perspective, it is possible to see the majority of priestly rituals as operating from magical premises. Contra both Kaufmann and Milgrom, magic is not antithetical to monotheism but in fact an intrinsic aspect of Israelite religion and cultic practice. As Levine suggests, "expiation as a ritual complex contained a

---

[263] Wright, *The Disposal of Impurity*, p. 69.

[264] The laying of hands on a sacrificial animal is a common element in many Priestly rituals of sacrifice, but there is no scholarly consensus with respect to its meaning or function. D. P. Wright ("The Gesture of Hand Placement in the Hebrew Bible and in Hittite Literature," *JAOS* 106 [1986], pp. 433–46) suggests that the general rite of laying *one* hand merely signified that the animal belonged to the owner. As Anderson ("Sacrifice," *The Anchor Bible Dictionary*) points out, "The exceptional act of laying on *two* hands on the day of atonement must be explained differently. In this case, the act of laying on hands identified a particular animal as the recipient of the ritual action."

magical component …. Such magic was not in contradiction to the biblical conception of God."[265]

In fact, magic is *intrinsic* to the biblical understanding of the relationship between Yahweh and his people. Sacrifices performed for the purpose of removing ritual impurity operate on a magical premise. In the Bible, impurity arises out of the bodily conditions and sins of the people rather than from the presence of other divine beings. This is an exception in the ancient Near East, where the majority of other religions consider demonic presence to accompany corpses and certain bodily discharges and diseases, or consider demons as the source of evils and impurities.[266] However, whatever its origin, the exorcism of evil requires a similar process and underlying premise in Mesopotamian, Hittite, and Israelite texts alike: unexpiated impurity pollutes the land and brings calamity to the people. To avert divine wrath, sacrifices and other cultic rituals must be performed.

Examples of this mentality outside of Israel include a prayer of the Hittite king Mursilis to the Hattian storm god in which he laments that a plague that had broken out during the reign of his father had continued unabated in his own reign. Upon inquiry, the storm god revealed through an oracle that violation of a sworn agreement with the Egyptians was the basis for the divine punishment. Restitution and confession were needed to expiate the crime perpetrated by the Hittites during his father's reign.[267] In the Bible as well, the sinner incurs guilt through transgression and "carries" (*ns'*; *sbl*) that guilt until it is removed by the performance of the proper rituals and sacrifices.

---

[265] Levine, pp. 90-91. We disagree with Levine's suggestion, however, that the "magical component" of sacrifice "related primarily to the particular utilization of sacrificial blood" and his attendant explanation and commentary. We also disagree that magic in Israelite ritual served to combat "the reality of anti-God forces." Such reconstructions of ancient Israelite beliefs are simply not substantiated by a straightforward reading of the biblical text. The presence of magic in the operant premises of Israelite sacrifice is tied rather to the mentality and worldview relating to the ability of ritual to effect results for which no physical causal connection was apparent.

[266] In the ancient Near East, "Impurity was feared because it was considered demonic. It was an unending threat to the gods themselves and especially to their temples, as exemplified by the images of protector gods set up before temple entrances … and, above all, by the elaborate cathartic and apotropaic rites to rid buildings of demons and prevent their return. Thus for both Israel and her neighbors impurity was a physical substance …. Israel thoroughly overhauled this concept of impurity in adapting it to its monotheistic system, but the notion of its dynamic and malefic power, especially in regard to the sancta, was not completely expunged from the Priestly Code" Milgrom *Cult and Conscience: The ASHAM and the Priestly Doctrine of Repentance* (Leiden: Brill, 1976) p. 392. See also Milgrom's "The Graduated ḤAṬṬA'T of Leviticus 5:1–13," *JAOS* 103 (1983), pp. 20-51; and D. P. Wright, *The Disposal of Impurity*, pp.129-46.

[267] See "Plague Prayers of Mursilis" in *ANET*, pp. 394–96; see also A. Malamat, "Doctrines of Causality in Hittite and Biblical Historiography: A Parallel," *VT* 5 (1955) pp. 1–12.

The argument could be made, however, that sacrificial ritual is intended as a *symbolic* and not magical elimination of sins: that the rituals are designed to lift the burden of sin psychologically from an individual, and the worshiper does not really believe that some sort of *physical* contamination has been removed. Analogy with the scapegoat ritual described above suggests otherwise. Further, in Num 19:20 and Lev 15:16-31, the sanctuary itself is described as being "defiled" because of ritual impurity from the unrepented guilt of individual Israelites. Such impurity pollutes a community like an aerial contaminant.[268] Individual violations against the holiness of God were likewise understood to pollute the land and bring the entire community under divine sanctions.[269] By polluting the land and defiling the residence and property of God, sin rendered the entire nation susceptible to calamity in the form of disease, famine, war, and other divine punishments. The system of expiatory sacrifice was designed to counteract this form of evil, and its premises are magical: atonement sacrifice cannot be perceived to be efficacious if the worshiper does not believe (a) that iniquity poses a physical threat to the individual and his community, and (b) in an unseen causal relationship between the action of sacrifice and the resultant absolution from sin.

Not all sacrifice is designed with atonement or purgation of sin as the desired outcome. The *šĕlāmîm* sacrifice, for example "was nothing more than an accepted manner for slaughtering any animal that was to be used for human consumption (Lev 17:1–7) in the P system."[270] Most discussions of biblical sacrifice understand a variety of meanings and purposes underlying and expressed by the practice:[271] covenant renewal, communion with God, providing a gift or food for the deity, demonstrating atonement and feelings of guilt for sins committed, and/or substituting the slaughter of an animal for the death of a sinner in order to expiate sin from the person offering the sacrifice.[272] Only the last explicitly employs a concept of magical transference similar to the premise of the scapegoat ritual.

---

[268] T. Frymer-Kensky, "Pollution, Purification, and Purgation in Biblical Israel" in *The Word of the Lord Shall Go Forth, Essays in Honor of David Noel Freedman*, eds. C. L. Meyers and M. O'Connor (Winona Lake: Eisenbrauns, 1983), pp. 399-414.

[269] See, for example, Num 35:33; cf. Jer 3:1-2, 9; Isa 24:5; Ps 106:38.

[270] G. Anderson, "Sacrifice," *The Anchor Bible Dictionary* (New York: Doubleday, 1992).

[271] See, for example, W. Robertson Smith, *Lectures on the Religion of the Semites*, 1884, reprint (New York: Ktav, 1969), pp. 269-388; R. Dussaud, *Les origines canaaneenes du sacrifice Israelite* (Paris: P. Geuthner, 1941), pp. 99-101; R. de Vaux, *Studies in Old Testament Sacrifice* (Cardiff: University of Wales Press, 1964); R. J. Thompson, *Penitence and Sacrifice in Early Israel outside the Levitical Law* (Leiden: Brill, 1963); and G. A. Anderson, *Sacrifices and Offerings in Ancient Israel, Studies in their Social and Political Importance* (Atlanta: Scholars Press, 1987).

[272] This last function of sacrifice is suggested in H. Gese, *Essays on Biblical Theology*, trans. K. Crim (Minneapolis: Augsburg, 1981).

Levine cites the examples of 1 Kings 18 (the contest at Mt. Carmel), Judges 6 (Gideon's altar), Judges 13 (the theophany to Manoah), and 2 Kings 3 (the Moabite king offering his firstborn) to argue that the *ʿōlāh* sacrifice should be understood as one designed to attract the deity's attention and invoke the deity's presence for a particular ritual occasion.[273] As Anderson points out, "such a theory would nicely explain the usage of the *ʿōlāh* for the purposes of divination when the deity's response to an urgent plea was desired, as in the case of Balaam's oracles (Numbers 21–24), or the usage of the *ʿōlāh* by Elijah as a means of testing which prophetic group truly 'had YHWH's attention' so to speak (1 Kings 18)."[274]

The magical premises of the *ʿōlāh* are therefore less evident than those concerned with atonement, such as the *ʾāšām* and the *ḥaṭṭāʾt* offerings. Milgrom has argued extensively for the purificatory role of blood in animal sacrifice.[275] He suggests that the blood purges the sanctum (not the sinner) from defilement, and this is why it is not applied to the sinner. This is exemplified in the *ḥaṭṭāʾt* offering required of those who experience "unclean" discharge:[276] "Thus you shall keep the people of Israel separate from their uncleanness in order that they not die in their uncleanness by defiling my tabernacle that is in their midst."[277] Impurity is thus conceived as "a physical substance, an aerial miasma which possessed magnetic attraction for the realm of the sacred."[278] The role of the purification offering is to remove this contaminating material from the sanctuary and the people in order to ensure the deity's continued patronage and the security of the community.

Thus the biblical evidence points to sacrificial rituals of atonement as designed to remove sin and impurity from the community, operating on the same premises as the scapegoat ritual: with no physical, causal connection between the action and the desired result. The underlying conception of the procedure and function of atonement or purgatory sacrifices is magical; magic remains at the heart of Israelite religious ritual. And in the Priestly text, the performance of magic is entirely the responsibility of priests. The kind of ritual magic that is mediated by priests is different from the performance of extraordinary supernatural acts of power by such figures as Elijah, which are what one would normally categorize as magic. For P, magic involves the manipulation of divine power on God's behalf for the proper administration of a community in which God dwells. To secure His con-

---

[273] Levine, *In the Presence of the Lord*, p. 24.

[274] Anderson, "Sacrifice."

[275] Milgrom, *Studies in Cultic Theology and Terminology* (Leiden: Brill, 1983).

[276] Anderson, "Sacrifice."

[277] Lev 15:31; cf. Num 19:13.

[278] Milgrom *Studies in Cultic Theology and Terminology*, p. 77.

tinued presence, the priests are empowered with the magical means to ensure constant purity in the community.

This explains why the performance of acts of magic by biblical heroes is downplayed in the Priestly text, and also why magical and divinatory abilities are so jealously guarded in Priestly legislation. The purpose of magic for P is primarily to avert God's anger by eliminating impurities and maintaining holiness in His community, and only Aaronid descendants are empowered with this awesome responsibility to mediate between the divine and human realms. There are no prophets in P because the idea that laity could communicate with God in other ways and even wield divine powers in the form of magic for their own ends is antithetical to the Priestly concept of the purpose of magic. It is detrimental and extremely threatening to P's entire worldview and its understanding of the nature of divine-human interaction. Thus in P it is most difficult to distinguish between the modern categories of "magic" and "religion": the religious mediation of priests is conceived in magical terms and founded upon a magical view of causation.

Blessings and Curses

The use of blessings and curses further demonstrates that this magical worldview pervades the works of all of the Tetrateuch's authors. It is not only common in biblical narrative but underlies many of the Psalms, the works of the prophets, and some of the wisdom literature.[279] Magic is the operant premise for the delivery of blessings and curses. Earlier studies of blessings and curses in the Hebrew Bible tended to distinguish between the "magical" and "religious" conceptions underlying each narrated case.[280] According to these studies, those benedictions or maledictions that operated by magic derived their power from a certain form of pronouncement, so that once spoken the blessing or curse must automatically bring

---

[279] A physical example of a blessing being employed for magical purposes comes from an excavated tomb at Ketef Ḥinnom, in which two silver amulets were found (see G. Barkay, *Ketef Ḥinnom: A Treasure Facing Jerusalem's Walls* [Jerusalem: The Israel Museum, 1986]). Once unrolled, the amulets revealed the earliest surviving inscription of a biblical text: the Priestly benediction from Num 6:24–27. The wearing of amulets and good-luck charms is a widespread phenomenon cross-culturally for the purpose of ensuring fortune and blessing. W. Propp (private communication) notes that the wording in Num 6:27, *wsmw 't šmy*, uses the image of an amulet apropos of the blessing: cf. Exod 28:12. On the Ketef Ḥinnom amulets as magical charms, see further W. G. Dever, *What Did the Biblical Writers Know and When did They Know It?* (Michigan: Eerdmans, 2001), p. 180.

[280] See J. Pedersen, *Der Eid bei den Semiten* (Strassburg: 1914); S. Mowinckel, *Segen und Fluch in Israels Kult und Psalmendichtung,* (Psalmenstudien, Kristiana: 1924), Repr. Amsterdam, 1961; J. Hempel, "Die israelitische Anschauungen von Segen und Fluch im Lichte altorientalischer Parallelen," *BZAW* 81:1961, pp. 30–113; and C. Westermann, *Blessing in the Bible and the Life of the Church,* trans. K. Crim (Philadelphia:1978).

about its intended result. By contrast, the "religious" conception attributed the efficacy of a blessing or curse to the cooperation of the deity invoked.

This distinction is difficult to substantiate with biblical evidence; the categories are neither explicit in the text, nor does there appear to be a difference in the minds of the authors between the blessings in which Yahweh is specifically named and those in which He is not. The nature of blessings and curses is rather to ask the gods to bring either benediction or malediction on the subject of the pronouncement; the notion of an "automatic" magical result as opposed to a divinely granted religious one makes too much of the subtle differences in the narrative techniques used to relate the stories. For example, the priest Eli blesses the barren Hannah, and Yahweh immediately fulfills the blessing by granting her a child.[281] When they dedicate Samuel to sanctuary service, Eli blesses both Hannah and Elkanah with more fertility, and the text again relates Yahweh's fulfillment of this blessing.[282] There is no indication that compulsion of the deity was involved, and the automatic result was attributed to God. In fact, in the example of Balaam in Numbers 22-24 discussed in Chapter Two, it demonstrates that God cannot be compelled in such matters; He will not *allow* Balaam to pronounce a curse against Israel, and when Balaam tries, a blessing emerges from his lips instead.

The mechanism by which blessings and curses operate is simply not elucidated in the Bible; speculations on whether certain forms of blessing and curse compel the deity whereas others propitiate Him are unwarranted and seek to categorize magic in opposition to religion on distinctly Frazerian lines.[283] As with atonement sacrifice, it is the concept underlying the practice that makes it magical: the belief that a desired effect can be brought about by an action that has no physical causal connection to the intended or actual result. The belief, for example, that the curse on the suspected *sôṭāh* will materialize only if she is indeed guilty is a belief in magic that exists at the heart of a "religious" priestly ritual.

The irrevocable power of a blessing is evident in Genesis 27, where Jacob deceives his father Isaac into bestowing the blessing of the firstborn onto himself rather than his brother Esau.[284] Isaac states that the one who received the blessing, regardless of its intention for another, "will in fact be blessed" (v 33). Esau begs his father to bless him also, but Isaac tells him "Your brother came with deception and took your blessing" (v 35). Isaac further informs Esau that, through the blessing he

---

[281] 1 Sam 1:17-20.

[282] 1 Sam 2:21-21.

[283] See our discussion in Chapter One.

[284] It is possible that blessings are irrevocable because they invoke the name of Yahweh (R. Friedman, private communication) either explicitly or implicitly. This would place the immutability of a blessing in the same category as the crime of "taking God's name in vain," the commandment against taking an oath in Yahweh's name and not fulfilling it (Exod 20:7).

has given to Jacob, Isaac has "made him [Esau's] superior" (v 37). Isaac is unable either to revoke his blessing of Jacob or to give the same (or even an equivalent) blessing to Esau, who is now doomed to serve his younger brother (v 40). Within the context of the story, the efficacy of this blessing will play itself out over the subsequent histories of the twin nations of Israel and Edom.

A curse is the opposite of a blessing, and taken just as seriously. In the story of Balaam in Numbers 22-24, the Moabites believe that the curse of a professional will empower them to defeat a people more numerous and powerful.[285] The biblical authors believed it too: they portray Yahweh as forbidding Balaam to curse Israel rather than attempt to demonstrate the ineffectual nature of such a curse. Israelite belief in the power of the curse is further evident not only in the abundance of laws against cursing, but in the fact that cursing one's parents, the handicapped, the king, or God, were all capital crimes.[286] In fact, ritual steps needed to be taken in order to avert the power of a curse. In the book of Judges, for example, Micah steals some silver protected by his mother's curse, and when he tells her she immediately responds by blessing Micah in the name of Yahweh and consecrating the silver to God.[287] Similarly, when Jonathan unknowingly brings his father Saul's curse upon himself, the people "ransomed" him to save him from ritual execution.[288]

This last example demonstrates the connection between oath and curse: in 1 Sam 14:26-7, Saul's curse is in the context of an oath that he swears. The swearing of an oath involved placing a curse on oneself or others, to be invoked if the oath should be broken. In the Bible, the believed effectiveness of a curse serves to convey the seriousness of certain oaths. In the example of 1 Samuel 14, Saul swears an oath that curses Jonathan and threatens his life. The king of Israel who swears to destroy Elisha in 2 Kgs 6:31 imprecates himself in his oath. Similarly, Jonathan includes a self-imprecation to guarantee his fidelity when he swears loyalty to David in 1 Sam 20:13. Abner also incorporates a self-curse when he swears an oath in the context of publicly switching allegiance from the family of Saul to David in 2 Sam 3:9.

There are numerous parallels in ancient Near Eastern texts. For example, at the core of most treaties was an oath (Akkadian *nīš ilī,* lit., "(by) the life of the gods") taken before the state deities of one or both parties. It was at the same time an imprecation (Akkadian *mamītu*), calling down divine wrath on the oath-

---

[285] Num 22:6.

[286] The law against cursing one's parents is mentioned in Exod 21:17 and Lev 20:19; the prohibition against cursing the handicapped is in Lev 19:14; cursing the king in 2 Samuel 16, and cursing God in Lev 24:11-24.

[287] Judg 17:1-3.

[288] 1 Sam 14:24–30, 36–45.

breaker. The deities before whom the oath was taken acted as guarantors of the treaty, punishing the one who transgressed it.[289] Hittite texts speak of the oath-gods "pursuing" (cf. Deut 28:45), "seizing," or "destroying" (Deut 28:20, 22) the oath-breaker. Assyrian documents likewise speak of the curse "overtaking" (cf. Deut 28:15, 45), "seizing," and "destroying."[290]

Many oaths were accompanied by the symbolic act of animal slaughter that made clear the force of the self-imprecation: if the oath-taker failed to fulfill that which he swore to do, he invoked the oath-curse and his fate would become that of the dismembered animal. A document from Alalakh in reference to a treaty reads: "Abban swore an oath to Yarimlim and cut the neck of a sheep, saying '(Let me so die) if I take back that which I gave you ....'"[291] The Sefire treaties likewise mention rituals that forecast the fate of the oath-breaker, including cutting a calf in two (cf. Jer 34:18).[292] At Mari "to kill an ass" (Akk *ḫāram qatālum*) became a technical expression for making a covenant.[293]

The power of blessings and curses does not seem to rely on the status of the person uttering them. They are neither restricted to the priesthood nor to prophets. There are, however, direct parallels between the way in which blessings and curses were believed to work and the premises upon which the priestly rituals described above operated. For example, there are certain rituals and gestures that often accompanied the pronouncement of blessings and curses. The laying on of hands (Gen 48:14) or the sharing of food and drink (Gen 14:18–20) might accompany a blessing. As we have seen, the self-imprecation involved in oath-taking was often symbolized by the dismemberment of animals.[294]

The Mosaic covenant at Sinai was likewise ratified by ritual sacrifice and a feast shared by both parties. After all of the laws are given to the people and they accept the covenant in principle (24:3), Moses builds an altar, offers sacrifices, and puts half of the blood on the altar. Then, once the people formally agree to the

---

[289] See D. Hillers, *Covenant: The History of a Biblical Idea* (Maryland: The Johns Hopkins Press, 1969), pp. 138-39.

[290] See D. J. McCarthy, *Treaty and Covenant: A Study in Form in the Ancient Oriental Documents and in the Old Testament* (Rome: Analecta Biblica 21A, 1978).

[291] D. J. Wiseman, "Abban and Alalaḫ,"*Journal of Cuneiform Studies* 12: 124–29; see also *ANET* pp. 532-3, 660.

[292] See *ANET* 659–61; J. A. Fitzmyer, *The Aramaic Inscriptions of Sefire* (Rome: Biblica et Orientalia 19, 1967); Hillers 1969, p. 139. Similar rites are mentioned in the treaty with Ashur-nirari V.

[293] McCarthy, *Treaty and Covenant*, p. 91.

[294] Cf. Gen 15:9-10, Jer 34:18-20, and 1 Sam 11:6-7. It is also possible that a similar curse was implied by the dismemberment of the concubine in Judg 19:29-30.

terms of the covenant (24:7), Moses throws the other half of the blood on the people, saying "Here is the blood of the covenant that Yahweh has made with you regarding all these things" (24:8). The sacrificial blood binds the two parties of the covenant (Yahweh, represented by the altar, and the people) and also signifies the curse implied by any oath: "The idea is similar to that involved in passing between the parts of an animal; the sprinkling with blood in a similar way establishes contact and identification with the victim."[295] Then Moses, Aaron, Nadab, Abihu and seventy of Israel's elders ascend the mountain to ratify the covenant by feasting with God (24:9-12).

The sacrifice and meal shared by both parties to a covenant are a common theme of Israel's neighbors as well. For example, in the context of sealing important legal transactions the Mari documents mention eating and drinking.[296] The Amarna Letters include one from the king of Egypt to his vassal king of Amurru, in which he reprimands his subject for having made a covenant with an enemy of the king by eating and drinking with him.[297] Other examples exist in the Bible as well. In Gen 26:26–33, Isaac and Abimelech make a pact in which both parties swear oaths, preceded the evening before by a feast prepared by Isaac. Another peace treaty with a related meal is described in Gen 31:43–54 between Jacob and Laban, where mutual nonaggression is combined with a stipulation forbidding Jacob to mistreat Laban's daughters or take additional wives.

As extensive scholarship has shown, the Sinai covenant itself closely modeled contemporary ancient Near Eastern suzerain-vassal treaties.[298] The oaths, blessings and curses that were integral to those treaties are equally apparent in the original presentation of the Mosaic covenant,[299] as well as in subsequent covenant renewal

---

[295] Hillers, *Covenant*, p. 57.

[296] *Archives Royales de Mari: transcriptions et traductions*, 8:13.

[297] Tell el-Amarna tablets, cited from J. A. Knudtzon, O. Weber, and E. Ebeling, *Die El-Amarna Tafeln*, 2 Vols. (VAB 2, Leipzig, 1915), 162:22-25.

[298] See G. E. Mendenhall, *Law and Covenant in Israel and the Ancient Near East* (Pittsburgh: Biblical Colloquium, 1955); and K. Baltzer, *The Covenant Formulary*, trans. D. E. Green (Philadelphia: Fortress Press, 1971); D. N. Freedman, "Divine Commitment and Human Obligation," *Interpretation* 18 (1964) 419-431; R. E. Friedman, "Torah and Covenant," *The Oxford Study Bible*, eds. M. J. Suggs, K. D. Sakenfeld, J. R. Mueller (New York: Oxford University Press, 1992); M. Weinfeld, "The Covenant of Grant in the Old Testament and in the Ancient Near East," *JAOS* 90 (1970) 184-203; P. Kalluveettil, *Declaration and Covenant: A Comprehensive Review of Covenant Formulae from the Old Testament and the Ancient Near East* (Rome: Analecta Biblica, 88:1982).

[299] See, for example, Deuteronomy 27-28. The Holiness Code also concludes with blessings (Leviticus 26:3–13) and curses (26:14–39) for observance or nonobservance of the laws therein. For studies comparing the biblical covenant blessings and curses with similar blessings and curses in ancient Near Eastern political treaties, see G. E. Mendenhall, *Law and*

and ratification ceremonies. A belief in magic is integral to the covenant at the foundation of Israel's nationhood because as we have seen, blessings and curses rely on a belief in a causal relationship between pronouncement of malediction or benediction and intended result. Curses were understood to be triggered by certain behaviors on the part of either the one pronouncing the curse, or the person who violated his oath and thereby invoked the self-curse understood by that oath. In the case of the suspected *śô̄ṭāh*, the curse only takes effect if the woman was indeed guilty of adultery.

The lack of physical connection between the action (blessing or curse) and its intended or actual result (good or bad fortune) places benediction, malediction, and attendant oath-taking and covenant-making within the purview of beliefs in magic. As we will see, the magical premises operant in the ideology of blessings and curses relating to covenant obligations suffuse the book of Deuteronomy as well as the Deuteronomistic History, injecting a particular kind of magical worldview directly into Israelite historiography, and exilic and postexilic theology.

The Magical Worldview in the Deuteronomistic History

Magic pervades Deuteronomy and the Deuteronomistic History in a slightly different way than in J, E, and P: magic in the DH informs the very structure of that history. The agenda of the historian is to explain Israel's history in terms of covenant. After detailing the statutes and ordinances Israel was to keep (Deut 5:12–26), Moses instructed the people to observe a ceremony at Shechem on Mounts Ebal and Gerizim, in which they would declare the curses or blessings that would come upon them for obedience or disobedience to those statutes and commandments (Deuteronomy 27–28). In Deuteronomy 30, Moses urges Israel to choose "life," "good," and "blessing" over "death," "evil," and the "curse" (vv 15, 19) by remaining loyal to Yahweh. Deuteronomy closes with the song of Moses, replete with elements of a covenant lawsuit (*rîb*) and the curse-induced evils that would come upon disobedient Israel.[300]

The Deuteronomist casts Israelite history in distinct terms: upholding the covenant brings blessings and prosperity, while violations and sin activate the curses and result in punishment. The continued occupation of the promised land

---

Covenant; K. Baltzer, *The Covenant Formulary*; D. J. McCarthy, *Treaty and Covenant*, 2d ed. (Rome: Analecta Biblica 21, 1978); D. R. Hillers, *Treaty-Curses and the Old Testament Prophets,* (Rome: Biblica et Orientalia 16, 1964); and J. D. Levenson, *Sinai and Zion* (Minneapolis: Winston Press, 1985).

[300] See G. E. Wright, "The Lawsuit of God: A Form-Critical Study of Deuteronomy 32," in *Israel's Prophetic Heritage*, eds. B. Anderson and W. Harrelson (New York: Harper, 1962).

depends entirely upon the people's observance of the law.[301] According to the historian, the sins of the period of the judges caused the shrinking of Israel's borders: the coastal area and the Lebanon (Josh 13:2–5; Judg 3:3) were taken away from the Israelites forever because of their sins (Josh 23:12; Judg 2:21–29). Later, the sins of the northern Israelites caused the loss of the territories of the north (2 Kgs 17:7–23). Finally, the fall of Jerusalem and the exile of Judah were brought about by the sins of Judah (2 Kgs 21:12–15).[302] The connection between behavior (sin) and consequence (exile) is a causal one with no physical connection between initiating action and result. The Sinai covenant frames the Deuteronomist's historical perspective. The history is one in which the covenant's curses have been invoked instead of its blessings, a fact patent to the historian. Thus the notion of covenant is integral to the Israelites' sense of nationhood: their obedience or disobedience to the covenant is what will dictate whether the covenant's blessings or curses will be enacted in their history. The Deuteronomistic historian demonstrates that through the Israelites' continual breach of covenant terms the curses were activated instead of the blessings.

In Deuteronomy 28, God tells the people that if they heed His commandments they will be blessed (v 1), and a list of blessings follows in vv 3-13.[303] In Deut 28:15, God tells the people that if they do not heed His commandments, they will be cursed. A long list of potential curses follows.[304] Deut 30:19 reiterates the underlying concept on which the covenant operates. This prefaces the Israelites' entry into the land and their future history within it: "I call the skies and the earth to witness regarding you today: I have placed life and death in front of you, blessing and curse." In this worldview it is up to the Israelites to choose their own fate, based on whether or not they live their lives in accordance with Yahweh's covenant to which the blessings and curses are attached.

Within the Deuteronomistic History the historian then demonstrates both the Israelites' breach of their covenant, and the realization of the curses listed in

---

[301] Cf. Deut 4:26; 11:17; 28:63; 30:19.

[302] See M. Weinfeld, *Zion* 49: 1984, pp. 115–37; and "The Extent of the Promised Land—The Status of Transjordan," in *Das Land Israel in biblischer Zeit,* ed. G. Strecker. Gottingen (1983) pp. 59–75.

[303] See Hillers, *Treaty-Curses*, pp. 43-79 for correlations between this list of blessings and standard treaty blessings in Mesopotamian and Hittite texts.

[304] It is worth noting that in v 46, Yahweh's covenant curses are designated to be *lĕʾōt ûlĕmôpēt* for Israel forever. The word *môpēt* is usually translated "wonder," and in most of its occurrences refers to the magical acts of Moses in Egypt (see Exod 4:21; 7:3, 9; 11:9, 10; Deut 4:34; 6:22; 7:19; 13:2, 3; 26:8; 29:2; 34:11; Jer 32:20, 21; Ps 78:43; 105:27; 135:9). Thus the covenant curses are understood to be "wonders" in the same way as Moses' magical acts: consequences of initiating actions that are not physically connected to those actions and therefore defy conventional explanation.

Deuteronomy 28. For example, the horrible curse in Deut 28:53, that in a state of extreme famine brought on by a siege parents will eat the flesh of their own children to stay alive, is reported in 2 Kgs 6:25-29 during the Aramaean siege of Samaria. The curse of not being buried properly, of one's carcass becoming food for birds and animals (Deut 28:26), happens precisely to Jezebel (2 Kgs 9:33-37), the queen responsible for actively promoting apostasy in Israel. The curse of having one's produce and animals stolen (Deut 28:30-33) comes true in 2 Kgs 24:2 when raiding bands make incursions against Judah. The tragic fate of Zedekiah in 2 Kgs 25:7, of having his children slaughtered in front of him just before he is blinded and led away in fetters to Babylon, combines a variety of curses from the list in Deuteronomy 28:   vv 28-29 that predict madness and blindness; v 48 forecasts the yoke around the treaty-violator's neck and v 49 tells of the coming of a nation from the end of the earth whose language will be foreign and whose manner will be oppressive and destructive. Most of Deut 28:30-51, 63-67 foretells the effects of the exile (cf. 2 Kgs 24-25). And the final curse is the capstone of the list: "Yahweh will bring you back to Egypt … and you will sell yourselves there to your enemies as slaves and as maids, and no one will buy" (v 68). Second Kings 25:26 relates that "All the people, from the least to the greatest … got up and came to Egypt" (cf. Jer 43:5-7).[305]

The pronouncement and subsequent implementation of blessings and curses relating to the covenant between Yahweh and Israel is central to the entire Deuteronomic work. It is the focus of the Deuteronomists' historiographic agenda. And its fundamental premise is a magical one: the actions of the individual have consequences relating to the fate of the entire community. The idea that sinful behavior has direct bearing on one's destiny is present in P and underlies the theology of sacrificial atonement. This magical understanding of the consequences of one's actions is also instrumental in the employment of blessings and curses in ancient Near Eastern covenant formularies. It is the Deuteronomistic Historian who takes this magical perspective to its logical conclusion, applying it to unlocking the mystery of Israel's fate. How could Yahweh allow His people to be exiled from their land, the Davidic dynasty to be cut off from its throne, and the place where Yahweh caused His name to dwell to be destroyed? Examining their history in terms of the magical power of blessings and curses revealed that there was no mystery at all. In repeatedly violating their covenant with Yahweh, Israel activated the covenant's curses instead of its blessings. Israel is responsible for bringing calamity on herself: the sins of individuals within the Deuteronomistic history lead directly to the dire consequences for the entire nation at the end of that history. There is no physical causal connection between sin and exile; this perspective on history makes sense only if one understands the magical worldview that underlies it.

---

[305] R. E. Friedman points out that the last curse in this list describes the events of the last page of the book of Kings, and yet "incredibly, this fact is almost never mentioned in commentaries on Deuteronomy or Kings or in biblical scholarship in general …. It is time that we recognized … the full horror of the final curse of the covenant" (*Commentary*, p. 653).

Conclusions

In this chapter we have seen that the place of magic in the Bible is not restricted to the tales of the extraordinary individuals whose acts of power help shape the history of Israel. Magic is implicit in Israelite religious expression, ritual, and self-understanding. Although it may be employed for these purposes, the use of magic is not simply a device of the storyteller to advance the plot, to demonstrate the divine favor shown to a particular man, or to showcase the power of Yahweh. Rather, belief in magic pervades the Israelite worldview. It is an intrinsic aspect of the way in which the universe is understood to operate. The relationship between humans and the divine is mediated by magic, and the correspondence between human actions and their divinely-dispatched consequences is a magical one. The lives of both individuals and communities are understood to unfold based on a magical correlation between actions and reactions: sin begets punishment, good works deserve divine reward. There is no physical, causal connection between behavior and fortune; subscribing to this type of worldview means believing in magic. The idea that God rewards the righteous and punishes the unjust in ways that manifest tangibly in the lives both of individuals and the community that is collectively responsible for the behavior of its constituents is a belief in magic. We turn to a discussion of these conclusions and implications in Chapter Five.

The Magic of Religion in Ancient Israel

Defining Magic

We began our investigation into the relationship between magic and religion in ancient Israel by addressing the problems inherent in trying to define magic in scholarly terms, and applying that definition to a place and time far removed from our own. It is important that the definition accord with both ancient and current sensibilities of what the term signifies. Additionally, we argued against adopting a purely social definition on the grounds that even when the term is used to classify foreign behaviors in opposition to one's own ("what you do is magic, what I do is religion"), the category should always refer to substance: an *act* is being performed. We also proposed that a definition of magic applicable to ancient Israel should adopt both an insider's (emic) and an outsider's (etic) perspective, and we defined magic as "an act performed by a person, with or without attribution to God, that has no physical, causal connection to the expected or actual results." This seems to be the kind of activity to which scholars are referring when they use the term "magic."

Successfully applying this definition to activities portrayed in the Hebrew Bible is complicated by several factors, including our cultural and temporal distance, theological implications, and the existence of numerous terms describing behavior we would classify as "magic" without one general Hebrew word applied in all situations. Our analysis of the vocabulary of magic yielded some important findings, however. We discovered that all of the prohibited activities listed in the Law Code and the Holiness Code had etymologies that betrayed foreign influence. The illegal activities of divination and sorcery were all behaviors in which Israel's neighbors engaged. By examining these prohibitions in the greater context of biblical narrative, we saw that the Israelite belief system supported the idea that such magic and divination actually worked. Additionally, though it was illegal in Israel, there was no condemnation attached to these activities on the part of foreigners. Lastly, we attempted to discover why magic and divination were prohibited in Deuteronomy 18 and Leviticus 19-20 when elsewhere in the Bible Israelite heroes were portrayed as wielding such powers. A closer look at the Deuteronomic Law Code and its immediate context showed that prophecy is offered as a legal alternative to sorcery and divination. The Holiness Code does not explicitly suggest any alternatives, declaring that the only viable means of communicating with the divine realm is through the priests.

Four conclusions can be drawn from this. First, magic as a category in a modern, overarching sense was not illegal in ancient Israel. Specifically, magic in the Hebrew Bible refers to the mediation of divine power; and in the hands of priests and prophets it is perfectly legal. Indeed, in Chapters Three and Four we explored the legal magic of Israelite prophets and priests. Second, the laws that prohibit certain activities on the part of laypeople are designed to restrict divine mediation to professional groups: prophets in the case of the Deuteronomic Law Code, and priests for the Holiness Code. Third, our definition of magic has an emic correspondence to the magical activities listed in the legal literature, as well as those portrayed neutrally as being engaged in by foreign "magicians": all of the terms we examined in Chapter Two concern activities with no physical, causal connection between initiating actions and intended results.

Thus, the social aspect of terms relating to magic is very important: the illegal activities listed in Deuteronomy and Leviticus are prohibited entirely on social grounds. The terms themselves, however, refer to substance: they correspond to actual magical practitioners and specialists who could do things that ordinary people could not. Thus when applied to ancient Israel the term "magic" is not just a social designation. The fourth conclusion then, is that contrary to findings from the New Testament, ancient Greek, Roman, and Rabbinic literature, the presumed dichotomy between magic and religion in ancient Israel cannot be upheld on purely social grounds. The issue is far more complicated, due to the diverse authorial perspectives represented within biblical literature.

Source Criticism

Portrayals of magic vary significantly among the biblical sources. This was apparent first in our examination of the legal material: although many of the same activities were deemed illegal, examining the context of these prohibitions revealed different motivations on the part of the authors of the Deuteronomic Law Code and the Holiness Code. Both were concerned with limiting divine interaction to a particular professional group. Although the Deuteronomic Law Code makes allowances for both priests and prophets, the Holiness Code restricts mediation between the sacred and the profane to priests alone.

Expanding our analysis to narrative texts in the Tetrateuch revealed further differences among the sources. The Priestly author takes great care to portray as few magical acts as possible, only telling stories about Moses' magic when there were antecedent stories from J or E that the author of P cannot ignore. P recasts these stories to show that Moses does not wield any magical power in his own right; rather he carries out explicit step-by-step instructions from Yahweh. This is most evident in the plague narratives. As often as possible, P has Aaron, the high priest, actually carry out the instructions instead of Moses. Most tellingly, P rewrites the Exodus 17 story of drawing water from a rock in Numbers 20. In the P version, because Moses appears to take credit for the miracle himself and uses Aaron's staff, he and Aaron receive the ultimate punishment of being forbidden to enter the Promised Land.

Writing after E and J, the author of P had to reconcile a written tradition of Moses as wonder-worker with the priestly laws that forbade magic by laypeople and ignored the existence of prophecy as a viable alternative. In contrast, the author of J was not restricted in his portrayal of magic. The difference between P and J in this regard is most evident in their parallel versions of challenges to Moses' authority in Numbers 16. In J, the issue is Moses' authority as Yahweh's representative and rightful leader of the people. Moses answers the challenge by calling, in the name of Yahweh, for the ground to open up and swallow the dissenters (vv 28-30). In the P version, the challenge issued to Moses and Aaron is to their exclusive right to the priesthood. Neither Moses nor Aaron acts against the challengers; rather, Yahweh sends fire to consume them, and this act unequivocally decides the issue.

The JE text also relates Balaam's magical abilities in Numbers 22-24 with no condemnation. In J, Joshua causes the sun to stop its motion, brings down the walls of Jericho, and parts the Jordan River to lead the Israelites across. He is neither a priest nor a prophet; the author of J was not concerned with limiting magical ability to people of a certain status.

The author of E also narrates many magical occurrences but promotes the idea more explicitly than J that magic both legitimates representatives of Yahweh and demonstrates Yahweh's power. As in P, the plague accounts in E follow a pattern of instructions given by Yahweh and carried out by Moses. However, the directions to Moses are first to prophesy to Pharaoh and then, upon Pharaoh's refusal, to bring about the plagues. The E text has a definite interest in prophets as the group to whom magical ability has been granted. The episode in Exodus 4 relates that the possession of magical power is a gift from God intended to function as a sign that the person who wields it has been chosen as Yahweh's representative. For E, magic designates the bearer as a true prophet.

The Deuteronomist disagrees and cautions specifically against believing the messages of a prophet simply on the basis of his ability to perform signs and wonders (Deut 13:2-4). However, in the Deuteronomic Law Code prophets are Israel's only viable non-priestly means of communicating with the divine realm; other methods, though effective, derive from foreign influence and are therefore illegal. D's attitude toward magic is ambiguous. The idea in the Deuteronomic Law Code that magic derives from foreign influences and occasioned the dispossession of previous occupants of the land by Yahweh lends a cautionary note to D's partial endorsement of it on the part of Israelite prophets. The author believes in its effectiveness but is concerned that it poses a threat to Israel's religion: the D text seems to recognize that non-priests and non-prophets might wield magical power and be taken as legitimate divine representatives when in fact they are not. Since one can wield this supernatural power without being a true representative of Yahweh, magic poses a dangerous threat to official Israelite religion.

On the other hand, the Deuteronomistic Historian is not reluctant to showcase magic in the narratives of his sources. In fact, the majority of biblical stories about magical acts centers on the figures of Elijah and Elisha. Additionally, as we saw in Chapter Four, the entire Deuteronomistic worldview is a magical one. The historian's notion of Israelite history is that it unfolds according to whether or not the behavior of the community conforms to its covenant promises.

Notwithstanding all of its restrictions on magic in the hands of laypeople, the Priestly worldview is also founded on beliefs in magic. If magic is an act that has no physical causal connection to its intended result, then many priestly rituals are essentially magical. In this light we examined the rites of the suspected *śôṭāh*, the scapegoat, and atonement sacrifice, and determined that official Israelite religion cannot be separated from a fundamental belief in magic.

It is interesting that D and P contain legal codes that attempt to distinguish illegitimate magic from cultic ritual, i.e. "magic" from "religion." Yet the perspective offered by a substantive and not merely social definition of magic reveals a worldview in their stories and rituals that is essentially a magical one. These sources represent attempts in ancient Israel to create a distinction between magic and religion on a purely social basis: what we do is religion, what you do is magic. This dichotomy is largely absent in the earlier authors, although intimated in the E text's emphasis on prophets.

Comparative Material

Thus we find a variety of perspectives on magic in the Hebrew Bible, reflecting both a diachronic change in Israel's perception of magic and a synchronic difference among the authors according to their status and vested interests in the cult. The assumption of the existence in biblical Israel of a firm distinction between religion and magic of the type found in literature of the Greek and Roman periods is not valid. In Chapter One we suggested that Egypt and Mesopotamia might offer better models for understanding biblical attitudes toward magic.

In Egypt, magic (*heka*) was conceived as a divine power, personified and yet amorphous, underlying all causality. It could be used by both gods and humans, within and outside of the official religious cult. Magic was an essential and inseparable aspect of Egyptian religion; priest and magician were often one and the same. This suggests a notion similar to the place of magic in the Israelite cult according to P. While P was moving toward the restriction of magic to priests alone, the underlying sense of what "magic" is differs between the two cultures. In Egypt, there was a special term to denote the power of magic, *heka*; there is no analogous word in Biblical Hebrew. The Egyptian concept of *heka* as both a deity and a supernatural power constantly active in the natural world likewise has no analogy in biblical conceptions. According to the biblical authors, the only active power in the world was Yahweh, and while He was usually acknowledged as the source of all causation and specifically of human magic, God was never understood as "magic" or "causality" personified.[306] Certainly the notion that His power could be used at will by anyone who knew how to manipulate it, is entirely absent in all biblical sources. Even Elijah and Elisha were portrayed as wielding magical powers as a consequence of having been chosen by Yahweh to be His messengers. Yahweh confers His power by His own choice; in Egypt, *heka* could be used by anyone who could read a spell book.

On the other hand, the incorporation of magical notions of causation into the Israelite worldview, self-understanding, and the explanation of historical events evident particularly in the Deuteronomistic History does show a similarity of belief with Egypt in the possibility of both natural and supernatural causes. Historiography in the contemporary world would not attribute the fall of a nation-state to its moral iniquity or breach of covenant with its patron deity. This is due to a worldview which implicitly distinguishes between the "natural" – events for which there is a physical, causal connection between action and result – and the "supernatural" for which no such explanation exists. Not only do we distinguish between the two, but we automatically reject the possibility of the latter, always seeking a plausible scientific, physical, *natural* explanation for a historical series of occurrences.

That is not to say that in biblical Israel and ancient Egypt no such distinction was present in their worldviews. They could certainly recognize the difference between the ordinary patterns of the tide and the unusual act of parting a sea, for example. They believed that certain people could wield extraordinary ("supernatural") powers and others could not. For instance, Elijah was understood to be able to withhold or produce rain in the name of Yahweh. Ahab could not do so, only because Yahweh had not chosen him as a prophet and divine representative. As the ancients were unable to rely on modern notions of physics, it is difficult to posit our sense of "natural" vs. "supernatural" for the ancient world. Rather, their distinctions would be better understood as "ordinary," i.e. conforming to a normal pattern of events, vs. "extraordinary."

Egypt thus serves as an interesting contrastive model for ancient Israel on a synchronic level. There is no evidence for major diachronic changes in the status of magical practitioners and practices in Egypt. Mesopotamia, however, offers better comparative evidence for understanding differences among the biblical authors with respect to the status of magic in ancient Israel. As in Egypt, distinctions between religion and magic are difficult to make; the main professional magicians in the Standard Babylonian period were priests. The *āšipu* was

---

[306] Although as W. Propp points out (private communication), the Hebrew word *yahweh* could be understood to mean "he causes to be," perhaps suggesting a similar underlying concept in Israel's original conception of God.

an exorcist, a magician, and usually a member of the temple personnel who hired himself out to private clients. The magic of the non-professional magician, known as the *kaššāp(t)u*, came to be seen as illegitimate and even demonic over time. With the rise of imperial urban contexts and official, temple-centered religion, Mesopotamian texts document a gradual trend toward the de-legitimation of magic in the hands of anyone other than the temple-affiliated *āšipu*.

Substantively, magic was used in Mesopotamia toward similar ends as in Egypt: to treat a variety of medical problems, end droughts, curse enemies, ensure fertility, and a host of other purposes. This common use of magic demonstrates a similar belief in causal connection between events even when no physical link is present. The inextricability of magical practice and religious ritual is likewise ubiquitous in the ancient Near East. Mesopotamia serves as a better model for understanding Israelite magic and religion than Egypt, however, because of changing attitudes toward the legitimacy of the use of magic outside temple-affiliated clergy attested by documents from different time periods. Although we do not possess a similar variety of texts with which to document diachronic change in ancient Israel, the sources incorporated into the Hebrew Bible do attest to a changing attitude toward magic.

In Egypt, Mesopotamia, and Israel, magic and religion originated as part of the same belief system. In Mesopotamia and Israel, a distinction between the two was forged gradually, over time, and this distinction was not based on substantive differences but rather on who could legitimately mediate divine power. As the priests grew in power and became the sole intercessors for the gods in elaborate temple complexes and rituals, they demonized the use of divine power in the hands of outsiders.

In light of this, it is significant that the profession of the *āšipu* was an in-herited one, passed down through the generations of particular families,[307] just as the priesthood could not be extended beyond the Aaronid clan according to the P text. The fact that the magic of foreigners was not condemned in the Bible and was even perceived as efficacious provides further evidence that the limitations on who could perform magic in Israel were primarily motivated by a social desire for a priestly monopoly. Thus substantively there was no difference between the underlying belief system of what we would term "magic" and "religion." Rather, the difference became a social one, over time. In the Bible, the Deuteronomic Law Code attempts to impose a purely social distinction in restricting divine mediation to prophets and priests. The P texts are more severe in their limits, imposing the death penalty for lay magicians and diviners, and not acknowledging the legitimacy of prophecy. In P, a social distinction is implicit

---

[307] W. Farber, "Witchcraft, Magic, and Divination in Ancient Mesopotamia" in *Civilizations of the Ancient Near East*, ed. J. Sasson (New York: Scribner, 1995), pp. 1895-1909.

in the promotion of priestly methods of divine intercession and the simultaneous prohibition of lay magicians and diviners.

Nineteenth-century anthropological models, laden with theological biases intent on demonstrating a positivist evolution from paganism to Protestantism, lacked the proper perspective from which to view the connection between magic and religion. Newer anthropological studies on the common origin of magic and religion in the phenomenon of shamanism provide a more fruitful approach to an understanding of the relationship between magic and religion. Anthropologists such as Winkelman, La Barre, and Driver[308] document the bifurcation of magical and religious specialists from the original figure of the shaman with the rise of more complex urban societies. The corresponding rise in the power of temple specialists affiliated with the governing powers leads to the marginalization and demonization of other professional mediators of divine power. Gradually, priests become the only legitimate intercessors between the realms of the sacred and the profane.

This is the situation that develops over time in Mesopotamia and in Israel. It is to be expected that with further complexity, the enlargement of empires, and the reality of daily multicultural contact, distinctions between magic and religion move from being implicit to becoming explicit, based solely on social distinctions. Texts from classical Greece, Rome, the New Testament, and Rabbinic literature attest to this next phase in the division between magic and religion.

The Magic of Religion

Recognizing the variety of perspectives represented by the different sources in the Hebrew Bible, in conjunction with a new understanding of the common origin of magic and religion in shamanism, leads to an appreciation of the similarities and differences between the Israelite worldview and that of its neighbors. We have noted that the variety of authors in the Hebrew Bible represents different stages of a movement away from shamanism toward organized temple-centered religion in a trend quite similar to that documented in Mesopotamia. Thus it is not surprising to find magical events at the foundation of the Israelite nation, magical beliefs at the core of religious rituals, and a magical worldview embedded in Israelite historiography. Despite the legal prohibitions, magic was not a foreign import to Israelite religion, but essential to it at every stage of development.

Notwithstanding similar trends over time, our analysis has also revealed that even though magic is as essential to the Israelite worldview as it was to its neighbors' there are important differences. A vast number of magical incanta-

---

[308] See the Introduction for these and other references.

tion and descriptive texts has survived from ancient Mesopotamia and Egypt, and attests to the use of magic to treat every conceivable problem, from toothaches to crying babies.[309] The only comparable magical texts for ancient Israel are the rituals prescribed for the *śôṭāh* and the scapegoat, both of which have been incorporated into legal contexts and their magical nature muted. This marks a radical difference in biblical attitudes with respect to the appropriate use and context for the employment of magic.

Throughout the ancient Near East (including Israel), magic involves communication between the natural and supernatural worlds, the human and divine realms. The way in which the divine realm is conceived thus impacts the way in which magic is used. In a polytheistic environment, in which many gods, spirits, and demons are believed to influence the course of events in the human realm both beneficently and maleficently, an abundance of magical rituals is required to ward off the many forms of evil. Different ills were understood to derive from different gods, spirits, demons, and curses, and thus required different spells and incantations with which to eliminate them.

In the official Israelite cult's emphasis on only one God, there was no need for a variety of means to exorcize different forms of evil. As emphasized by Kaufmann and Milgrom, evil came to be understood as a product of *human* impurity rather than demonic influence. Therefore a large corpus of incantatory material was unnecessary; there developed instead a body of laws relating to strict divisions between purity and impurity, and the means by which Israelites could propitiate Yahweh to remove their impurity and thereby eliminate evil.

The emphasis on only one God also led to a priesthood even more jealously guarded than in Mesopotamia. With one God, there could only be one legitimate temple, and one family of priests instead of the several families of *āšipu* attested in Mesopotamia for their different temples. The question of when monotheism originated in ancient Israel is not easily answered; however, by the time of the authorship of the Priestly text, the concept of only one God had deeply impacted the place of magic in Israelite religion.

The fact that a magical worldview persisted and remained at the heart of biblical religious ritual and history has significant implications for the development of Judaism and Christianity out of the biblical context. The concepts of sin and punishment, blessing and curse, and sacrifice are intrinsic to the religious beliefs of both biblically-based religions. As Rabbinic and New Testament scholars have noted, magical beliefs persist in the post-biblical period despite the dawn of self-conscious distinctions between magic and religion. The application of a substantive definition of magic to our examination of biblical religion

---

[309] See W. Farber, *Schlaf, Kindschen, schlaf!: Mesopotamische baby-Beschwörungen und - Rituale* (Indiana: Eisenbrauns, 1989); J. F. Borghouts, *Ancient Egyptian Magical Texts* (Leiden: Brill, 1978); and *ANET*, pp. 100-101.

has revealed the inextricability of these two concepts in the ancient worldview. However, according to our definition of magic, Jewish and Christian religious beliefs also necessarily retain a magical worldview at their essence. Perhaps it is not possible to have a religion without a fundamentally magical worldview. Would we believe in the founder of a religion if he could not mediate between the divine and human realms? It would seem that as long as we believe that there are separate divine and human realms, that communication is possible between the two, and that events in our realm that lack a physical causal explanation can be attributed to the intervention of the divine, our religions retain a sense of magic at their core.

Bibliography

Abusch, T., and K. Van der Toorn, *Mesopotamian Magic: Textual, Historical, and Interpretative Perspectives.* Groningen: Styx Publications, 1999.

_____. "Witchcraft and the Anger of the Personal God" in *Mesopotamian Magic: Textual, Historical, and Interpretative Perspectives.* Eds. T. Abusch and K. van der Toorn. Groningen: Styx Publications, 1999.

_____. "The Socio-Religious Framework of the Babylonian Witchcraft Ceremony *Maqlu*: Some Observations on the Introductory Section of the Text, Part II," *Solving Riddles and Untying Knots. Biblical, Epigraphic, and Semitic Studies in Honor of Jonas C. Greenfield.* Z. Zevit, S. Gitin, M. Sokoloff, eds. Winona Lake: Eisenbrauns, 1995, pp. 467-494.

_____. "The Demonic Image of the Witch in Standard Babylonian Literature," *Religion, Science and Magic In Concert and In Conflict*, eds. J. Neusner, E. S. Frerichs, P. V. McCracken Flesher. New York: Oxford University Press, 1989, pp. 27-58.

_____. *Babylonian Witchcraft Literature: Case Studies.* Brown Judaic Studies 132. Atlanta: Scholars Press, 1987.

_____. "Mesopotamian Anti-Witchcraft Literature: Texts and Studies" *JNES* 33 (1974) 251-62.

Ahlstrom, G. W. *Aspects of Syncretism in Israelite Religion.* Trans. E. J. Sharpe. Lund: Gleerup, 1963.

Albright, W. F. "An Aramean Magical Text in Hebrew from the Seventh Century B.C." *BASOR* 76 (1939), pp. 5-11.

_____. *Archaeology and the Religion of Israel.* Baltimore: Johns Hopkins, 1942.

_____. *From the Stone Age to Christianity: Monotheism and the Historical Process.* 2nd ed. New York: Doubleday, 1957.

Anderson, G. A. "Sacrifice," *The Anchor Bible Dictionary*, ed. D. N. Freedman. New York: Doubleday, 1992.

_____. *Sacrifices and Offerings in Ancient Israel, Studies in their Social and Political Importance.* Atlanta: Scholars Press, 1987.

Astour, M. "Two Ugaritic Serpent Charms." *JNES* 27 (1968), pp. 13-36.

Auerbach, E. *Mimesis.* Princeton, NJ: Princeton University Press, 1968.

Aune, D. E. "Magic in Early Christianity" *ANRW* II 23.2 (1980) 1507-1557.

Bach, A. "Viewing the Sotah (Numbers 5.11-31) as the Glass Half Empty and Wondering How to View It Half Full." *Women in the Hebrew Bible, A Reader.* Ed. A. Bach. New York: Routledge, 1999, pp. 503-522.

Baltzer, K. *The Covenant Formulary.* Trans. D. E. Green. Philadelphia: Fortress Press, 1971.

Barkay, G. *Ketef Hinnom: A Treasure Facing Jerusalem's Walls.* Jerusalem: The Israel Museum, 1986.

Benjamin, D. C. "An Anthropology of Prophecy" *Biblical Theology Bulletin* 21 (1991) 135-44.

Blythin, I. "Magic and Methodology." *Numen* 17 (1970), pp. 45-59.

Boadt, L. *Reading the Old Testament: An Introduction.* New York: Paulist Press, 1984.

Borghouts, J. F. *Ancient Egyptian Magical Texts.* Leiden: Brill, 1978.

Bottéro, J. "Les Morts et l'au-delà dans les rituels en accadien contre l'action des 'revenants,'" *ZAW* 73 (1983) pp. 153–203.

Braman, R. M. *The Problem of Magic in Ancient Israel: A century of studies.* Dissertation: Drew University, 1989.

Brichto, H.C. "The Case of the Sotah and a Reconsideration of Biblical Law." *HUCA* 46 (1975), pp. 55-70.

_____. *The Problem of 'Curse' in the Hebrew Bible.* Philadelphia: JBL Monograph Series 13, 1963.

Budd, P. J. *Numbers,* Word Bible Commentary 5; Waco, TX: Word, 1984.

Burden, J. "Magic and Divination in the Old Testament and their Relevance for the Church in Africa." *Missionalia* 1 (1973), pp. 103-111.

Caplice, R. *The Akkadian Namburbi Texts: An Introduction.* Los Angeles: Undena Publications, 1974.

Caquot, A. "La divination dans l'Ancien Israel" in *La Divination.* Eds. A. Caquot and M. Leibovici. Paris: Presses Universitaires de France, 1968, pp. 83-113.

Carr, D. M. *Reading the Fractures of Genesis: Historical and Literary Approaches.* Lousville: Westminster John Knox Press: 1996.

Clements, R. *Abraham and David.* London: SCM, 1967.

Coats, G. W. *Rebellion in the Wilderness.* Nashville: Abingdon, 1968.

Craigie, P. C. *The Book of Deuteronomy.* Grand Rapids: Eerdmans, 1976.

Crawford, T. G. *Blessing and Curse in Syro-Palestinian Inscriptions of the Iron Age,* American University Series, ser. VII, vol. 120. New York: P. Lang, 1992.

Crenshaw, J. L. *Prophetic Conflict: Its Effect upon Israelite Religion.* New York: Walter de Gruyter, 1971.

Cross, F. M. *Canaanite Myth and Hebrew Epic.* Cambridge: Harvard, 1973.

Cryer, F. H. *Divination in Ancient Israel and its Near Eastern Environment.* JSOTSup 142, Sheffield: JSOT Press, 1994.

Davies, T. W. *Magic, Divination and Demonology Among the Hebrews and their Neighbours.* London: J. Clarke and Co., 1898.

Dever, W. G. *What Did the Biblical Writers Know and When Did They Know It?* Michigan: Eerdmans, 2001.

Dhorme, E. "Pretres, devins et mages dans l'ancienne religion des Hebreux." *Revue d'Histoire des Religions* 108 (1933), pp. 113-133.

Douglas, M. *Purity and Danger.* London: Routledge and Kegan Paul, 1966; reprinted 1979.

_____. *Implicit Meanings: Essays in Anthropology.* London: Routledge and Kegan Paul, 1975.

_____. *Natural Symbols: Explorations in Cosmology.* New York: Pantheon Books, 1982 (reprint of 1970).

Driver, G. R. "Two problems in the Old Testament examined in the light of Assyriology." *Syria* 33 (1956).

Driver, S. R. *A Critical and Exegetical Commentary on Deuteronomy.* 3rd ed. Edinburgh: T. and T. Clark, 1895.

Driver, T. W. *The Magic of Ritual: Our Need for Liberating Rites that Transform our Lives and Our Communities.* New York: HarperCollins, 1991.

Durkheim, E. *The Elementary Forms of the Religious Life.* New York: The Macmillan Co., 1965; reprint of 1915.

Dussaud, R. *Les origines canaaneenes du sacrifice israelite.* Paris: P. Geuthner, 1941.

Ebeling, E. *Tod und Leben nach den Vorstellungen der Babylonier.* Berlin, 1931.

Eliade, M. *The Sacred and the Profane.* New York: Harcourt, 1959.

Engelhard, D. H. *Hittite Magical Practices: An Analysis.* Dissertation: Brandeis University, 1970.

Evans-Pritchard, E. E. *Witchcraft, Oracle and Magic.* Oxford: The Clarendon Press, 1937.

_____. *Theories of Primitive Religion.* Oxford: Clarendon Press, 1965.

Faraone, C. A. "Molten Wax, Spilt Wine and Mutilated Animals: Sympathetic Magic in Near Eastern and Early Greek Oath Ceremonies," *JHS* 113 (1993) 60-80.

Farber, W. "Witchcraft, Magic, and Divination in Ancient Mesopotamia" in *Civilizations of the Ancient Near East.* Ed. J. Sasson. New York: Scribner, 1995, pp. 1895-1909.

_____. *Schlaf, Kindschen, schlaf!: Mesopotamische baby-Beschwörungen und –Rituale.* Indiana: Eisenbrauns, 1989.

Finkelstein, J. J. "Hebrew hbr and Semitic *HBR." *JBL* 75 (1956) pp. 328-331.

Fishbane, M. "Accusations of Adultery: A Study of Law and Scribal Practice in Numbers 5:11-31." *HUCA* 45 (1974) pp. 25-45.

_____. *Studies in Biblical Magic: Origins, Uses and Transformations of Terminology and Literary Form.* Dissertation: Brandeis, 1971.

Fitzmyer, J. *The Aramaic Inscriptions of Sefire.* Rome: Biblica et Orientalia 19, 1967.

Flint, V. I. J. *The Rise of Magic in Early Medieval Europe.* Princeton: Princeton University Press, 1991.

Fohrer, G. "Prophetie und Magie," *ZAW* 78 (1966) 25-47.

Frankfurter, D. "The Magic of Writing and the Writing of Magic: The Power of the Word in Egyptian and Greek Traditions," *Helios* 21 (1994), 189-97.

Frazer, J. G. *The Golden Bough. Part 1, The Magic Art and the Evolution of Kings.* New York: the Macmillan Company, 1910.

Freedman, D. N. "Divine Commitment and Human Obligation." *Interpretation* 18 (1964): 419-431.

_____. and S. Dolansky Overton, "Omitting the Omissions: The Case for Haplography in the Transmission of the Biblical Texts," in *'Imagining'*

Biblical Worlds: Spatial, Social and Historical Constructs. Essays in Honor of James W. Flanagan. Eds. D. M. Gunn and P. M. McNutt. Sheffield, 2002, pp. 88-105.

Friedman, R. E. *Commentary on the Torah.* San Francisco: Harper, 2001.

_____. *The Hidden Book in the Bible.* San Francisco: Harper, 1998.

_____. *The Disappearance of God.* New York: Little, Brown and Co., 1995.

_____. *Who Wrote the Bible?* New York: Simon and Schuster, Summit, 1987.

_____. *The Exile and Biblical Narrative.* HSM 22, 1981.

_____. "Torah and Covenant," *The Oxford Study Bible.* Eds. M. J. Suggs, K. D. Sakenfeld, J. R. Mueller. New York: Oxford University Press, 1992.

_____., and S. Dolansky Overton. "Death and Afterlife: The Biblical Silence." *Judaism in Late Antiquity Part 4: Death, Life-After-Death, Resurrection and The World-to-Come in the Judaisms of Antiquity.* Eds. A. J. Avery-Peck and J. Neusner. Leiden: Brill, 1999, pp. 35-69.

Friedrich, I. *Ephod und Choschen im Lichte des Alten Orients.* Wien: Herder, 1968.

Frymer-Kensky, T. "The Strange Case of the Suspected Sota (Numbers v 11-31)," *VT* 34 (1984) 11-26.

_____. "Pollution, Purification, and Purgation in Biblical Israel." *The Word of the Lord Shall Go Forth, Essays in Honor of David Noel Freedman.* Eds. C. L. Meyers and M. O'Connor. Winona Lake: Eisenbrauns, 1983, pp.399-414.

_____. *The Judicial Ordeal in the Ancient Near East.* Dissertation: Yale University, 1977.

Gager, J. G. *Curse Tablets and Binding Spells from the Ancient World*, Oxford University Press, 1992.

_____. "Moses the Magician: Hero of an Ancient Counter-culture?" *Helios* 18.2 (1994), 179-188.

Garrett, S. R. "Light on a Dark Subject and Vice Versa: Magic and Magicians in the New Testament," *Religion, Science and Magic In Concert and In Conflict*, eds. J. Neusner, E. S. Frerichs, P. V. McCracken Flesher. New York: Oxford University Press, 1989, pp. 142-165.

Gaster, T. H. "A Canaanite Magical Text." *Orientalia* 11 (1942), pp. 41-79.

Gese, H. *Essays on Biblical Theology*, trans. K. Crim. Minneapolis: Augsburg, 1981.

Goldin, J. "The Magic of Magic and Superstition," *Aspects of Religious Propaganda in Judaism and Early Christianity*, E. Schuessler Fiorenza, ed., Notre Dame, 1976 pp. 113-147.

Good, E. M. *Irony in the Old Testament.* Sheffield: Almond Press, 1981.

Goode, W. J. "Magic and Religion: A Continuum," *Ethnos* 14 (1949) 172-182.

Grabbe, L. L. *Priests, Prophets, Diviners, Sages: A Socio-Historical Study of Religious Specialists in Ancient Israel.* Pennsylvania: Trinity Press, 1995.

Graf, F. *Magic in the Ancient World* (translated by F. Philip). Harvard University Press, 1997.

_____. "Excluding the Charming: The Development of the Greek Concept of Magic," *Ancient Magic and Ritual Power.* Eds. M. Meyer and P. Mirecki. Leiden: Brill, 1995, pp. 29-42.

Gray, J. *Numbers*, ICC: Edinburgh, 1903.

Gross, W. *Bileam: Literar- und formkritische Untersuchung der Prosa in Num 22–24.* Munich, 1974.

Guillaume, A. *Prophecy and Divination among the Hebrews and Other Semites.* London: Hodder and Stoughton, 1938.

Hackett, J. A. "Some Observations on the Balaam Tradition at Deir ʿAllā,ʷ *BA* 49 (1986) pp. 216–22.

Hammond, D. "Magic: A Problem in Semantics," *American Anthropologist* 72 (1970) 1349-56.

Harrelson, W. "The Religion of Ancient Israel." *Listening: Journal of Religion and Culture* 19 (1984), pp. 19-29.

Hempel, J. "Die israelitische Anschauungen von Segen und Fluch im Lichte altorientalischer Parallelen." *ZAW* 81 (1961): 30-113.

Hillers, D. R. *Covenant: The History of a Biblical Idea.* Maryland: The Johns Hopkins Press, 1969.

_____. *Micah.* Philadelphia: Fortress Press, 1984.

_____. *Treaty-Curses and the Old Testament Prophets.* Rome: Biblica et Orientalia 16, 1964.

Hoffner, H. A. Jr., "Hittite tarpis and Hebrew teraphim," *JNES* 27 (1968), pp. 61-68.

Holladay, W. L. *A Concise Hebrew and Aramaic Lexicon of the Old Testament.* Grand Rapids: Eerdmans, 1971.

Huffmon, H. B. "Priestly Divination in Israel," *The Word of the Lord Shall Go Forth, Essays in Honor of David Noel Freedman.* Eds. C. L. Meyers and M. O'Connor. Winona Lake: Eisenbrauns, 1983, pp. 355-358.

Hull, J. M. *Hellenistic Magic and the Synoptic Tradition.* London: SCM Press, 1974.

Iwry, S. "The Qumran Isaiah and the End of the Dial of Ahaz." *BASOR* 147 (1957), pp. 27-33.

_____. "New Evidence for Belomancy in Ancient Palestine and Phoenicia." *JAOS* 81 (1961), pp. 27-34.

Jeffers, A. *Magic and Divination in Ancient Palestine and Syria.* Leiden: Brill, 1996.

Kalluveettil, P. *Declaration and Covenant: A Comprehensive Review of Covenant Formulae from the Old Testament and the Ancient Near East.* Rome: Analecta Biblica, 88, 1982.

Kapelrud, A. S. "Shamanistic Features in the Old Testament" in *Studies in Shamanism*, ed. C.-M. Edsman. Stockholm: Almqvist and Wiskell, 1967, pp. 90-96.

_____. "The Interrelationship between Religion and Magic in Hittite Religion," *Numen* 6 (1959), pp. 32-50.

Kaufmann, Y. *Toledot ha'emunah hayisra'elit* (Tel Aviv: Bialik Institute-Dvir), Vols. 1-7 (1937-1948). Translated and abridged from the Hebrew by M. Greenberg as *The Religion of Israel* (Chicago: University of Chicago Press, 1960).

Kee, H. C. "Magic and Messiah" in *Religion, Science and Magic in Concert and in Conflict*. J. Neusner, E. S. Frerichs, P. V. McCracken Flesher. New York: Oxford University Press, 1989.

Keel, O. *Symbolism of the Biblical World*. London: SPCK, 1978.

Key, A. F. "The Magical Background of Is. 6:9-13." *JBL* 86 (1967), pp. 198-204.

Knudtzon, J. A., O. Weber, and E. Ebeling, *Die El-Amarna Tafeln*, 2 Vols. VAB 2, Leipzig, 1915.

Kohata, F. "Die priesterschriftlich Uberlieferungsgeschichte von Numeri XX 1-13," *Annual of the Japanese Biblical Institute* 3 (1977) pp. 3-34.

Kuemmerlin-McLean, J. *Divination and Magic in Ancient Israel*. Dissertation: Vanderbilt University, 1986.

LaBarre, Weston. *The Ghost Dance. Origins of Religion*. Illinois: Waveland Press, 1990.

Levenson, J. D. *Sinai and Zion*. Minneapolis: Winston Press, 1985.

Levine, B. L. *In the Presence of the Lord*. Leiden: Brill, 1974.

Lindblom, J. "Lot-casting in the Old Testament." *Vetus Testamentum* 12 (1962): 164-178.

_____. *Prophecy in Ancient Israel*. Philadelphia: Fortress, 1973.

Lods, A. "Le role des idees magiques dans la mentalite Israelite," in *Old Testament Essays* (London: C. Griffin, 1927) 55-76.

Long, B. O. "The Effect of Divination upon Israelite Literature." *JBL* 92 (1973), 489-97.

_____. "The Social Setting for Prophetic Miracle Stories," *Semeia* 3 (1975) 46-59.

Malamat, A. "Doctrines of Causality in Hittite and Biblical Historiography: A Parallel." *VT* 5 (1955) 1-12.

Malinowski, B. *Magic, Science and Religion and Other Essays*. New York: Doubleday, 1948.

_____. *A Scientific Theory of Culture and Other Essays*. New York: Oxford University Press, 1944.

Margaliot, M. "Het(') mose(h) we'aharon beme meriba," *Beth Mikra* 19 (1974), pp. 374-400.

Mauss, M. *A General Theory of Magic* (translated by R. Brain), London: Routledge and Kegan Paul, 1972.

Mayes, A. D. H. *Deuteronomy*. Grand Rapids: Eerdmans, 1979.

McCarter, P. Kyle, Jr. *I Samuel*. New York: Doubleday, 1980.

_____. *II Samuel*. New York: Doubleday, 1984.

McCarthy, D. J. *Treaty and Covenant: A Study in Form in the Ancient Oriental Documents and in the Old Testament*. Rome: Analecta Biblica 21A, 1978.

McKay, J. *Religion in Judah Under the Assyrians*. London: SCM Press Ltd, 1973.

Meier, G. "Die Beschworungssammlung Maqlu. *Archiv fur Orientforschung* (1937).

Mendenhall, G. E., *Law and Covenant in Israel and the Ancient Near East*. Pittsburgh: Biblical Colloquium, 1955.

_____. and G. A. Herion. "Covenant." *The Anchor Bible Dictionary*. Ed. D.N. Freedman. New York: Doubleday, 1992.

Merrifield, R. *The Archaeology of Ritual and Magic*. London: Batsford, 1987.

Meyer, M., and P. Mirecki, *Ancient Magic and Ritual Power* (Leiden: E.J. Brill, 1995).

Meyers, C. "Ephod." *The Anchor Bible Dictionary*. Ed. D.N. Freedman. New York: Doubleday, 1992.

Milgrom, J. *Leviticus 1-16*. The Anchor Bible Commentary Series. New York: Doubleday, 1991.

_____. *Numbers*. The JPS Torah Commentary. Philadelphia: Jewish Publication Society of America, 1990.

_____. *Studies in Cultic Theology and Terminology*. Leiden: Brill, 1983.

_____. "Magic, Monotheism and the Sin of Moses," *The Quest for the Kingdom of God: Studies in Honor of G. E. Mendenhall*. Eds. H. B. Huffmon, F. A. Spina and A. R. W. Green. Indiana: Eisenbrauns, 1983.

_____. "The Graduated *HATTAT* of Leviticus 5:1–13," *JAOS* 103 (1983): 20-51.

_____. "The Case of the Suspected Adulteress, Numbers 5.11-31: Redaction and Meaning," *The Creation of Sacred Literature*. Ed. R. E. Friedman. Berkeley: University of California Press, 1981.

_____. *Cult and Conscience*. Leiden: Brill, 1976.

Moor, J.C. de. *An Anthology of Religious Texts from Ugarit*. Leiden: Brill, 1987.

Mowinckel, S. *Segen und Fluch in Israels Kult und Psalmendichtung*. Kristiana: Psalmenstudien, 1924.

_____. *Erwagungen zur Pentateuch Quellenfrage*. Trondheim: Universitetsforlaget, 1964.

_____. "Der Ursprung der Bileamsage," *ZAW* 48 (1930), pp. 233–71.

Myhrman, D. "Die Labartu-Texte," *ZAW* 16 (1902): 141-200.

Naveh, J. and S. Shaked, *Magic Spells and Formulae*, Jerusalem, 1993.

_____., and S. Shaked, *Amulets and Magic Bowls*, Jerusalem, 1985.

Neusner, J. "Phenomenon of the Rabbi," *Numen* 16/1 (1969) 1-20.

_____., and E. S. Frerichs, P. V. McCracken Flesher, *Religion, Science and Magic: In Concert and in Conflict*. New York, Oxford University Press, 1989.

_____. "Science and Magic, Miracle and Magic in Formative Judaism: The System and the Difference," *Religion, Science and Magic in Concert and in Conflict*. Eds. J. Neusner, E. S. Frerichs and P. V. McCracken Flesher. New York: Oxford University Press, 1989.

Nigosian, S. A. "Anti-Divinatory Statements in Biblical Codes," *Theological Review* XVIII.1 (1997) 21-34.

Noegel, S. B. "Sex, Sticks, and the Trickster in Gen. 30:31-43," *JANES* 25 (1997) 7-17.

_____. "Moses and Magic: Notes on the Book of Exodus," *JANES* 24 (1996) 45-59.

Noth, M. *Numbers: a commentary*. Trans. James D. Martin. Philadelphia: Westminster Press, 1968.

O'Keefe, D. L. *Stolen Lightning: The Social Theory of Magic*. New York: Random House, 1982.

Oppenheim, A. L. *Ancient Mesopotamia*. Chicago: University of Chicago Press, 1964.

_____. *The Interpretation of Dreams in the Ancient Near East*. Philadelphia: 1956.

_____. "The Interpretation of Dreams," *Proceedings of the American Philosophical Society* 46 (1955).

Orlinsky, H. "The Seer Priest and the Prophet in Ancient Israel." *Essays in Biblical Culture and Bible Translation*. New York: KTAV, 1974, pp. 39-65.

Overholt, T. W. *Channels of Prophecy: The Social Dynamics of Prophetic Activity*. Minneapolis: Fortress Press, 1989.

Parker, S. B. "Possession, Trance and Prophecy in Pre-exilic Israel," *VT* 28 (1978), 271-285.

Parpola, S. *Letters from Assyrian Scholars to the Kings Esarhaddon and Assurbanipal*. Neukirchen/Vluyn: Kevelaer, 1971.

Pedersen, J. *Der Eid bei den Semiten*. Strassburg, 1914.

Pettersson, O. "Magic – Religion; Some marginal notes to an old problem," *Ethnos* 22 (1957) 109-119.

Polzin, R. *Late Biblical Hebrew: Toward an Historical Typology of Biblical Hebrew Prose*. HSM, Atlanta: Scholars Press, 1976.

Porter, J. R. "Ancient Israel," in *Divination and Oracles*, ed. M. Loewe and C. Blacker. London/Boston: Allen and Unwin, 1981.

Propp, W. H. *Exodus 1-18*. Anchor Bible. New York: Doubleday, 1999.

_____. "The Rod of Aaron and the Sin of Moses." *JBL* 107.1 (1988) 19-26.

Quaegebeur, J. "On the Egyptian Equivalent of Biblical *ḥarṭummîm*," in *Pharaonic Egypt, the Bible, and Christianity*. Ed. S. Israelit-Groll. Jerusalem, 1985, pp. 162-72.

Reik, T. *Pagan Rites in Judaism. From Sex Initiation, Magic, Moon Cult, Tattooing, Mutilation and Other Primitive Rituals to Family Loyalty and Solidarity*. New York: S. and C. Farrar, 1964.

Reiner, E. *Šurpu: A Collection of Sumerian and Akkadian Incantations.* Beiheft 11: Graz, 1958.

Remus, H. "Does Terminology Distinguish Early Christian from Pagan Miracles?" *JBL* 101 (1982), 531-51.

Rendtorff, R. *Die Gesetze in der Priesterschrift.* Gottingen, 1963.

Ricks, S. D. "The Magician as Outsider in the Hebrew Bible and the New Testament," *Ancient Magic and Ritual Power.* Eds. M. Meyer and P. Mirecki. Leiden: Brill, 1995.

Ritner, R. K. *The Mechanics of Ancient Egyptian Magical Practice*, Oriental Institute of the University of Chicago, 1993.

Ritter, E. K. "Magical-Expert (= āšipu) and Physician (=ûas)," in *Studies in Honor of Benno Landsberger.* Assyriological Studies 16: Chicago, 1965, pp. 299-321.

Robinson, H. Wheeler. *Inspiration and Revelation in the Old Testament.* Oxford: Blackwell, 1978.

Rogerson, J. *The Supernatural in the Old Testament.* Guildford and London: Lutterworth, 1976.

Rogerson, J. W. *Anthropology and the Old Testament*, Oxford 1978.

Rosenberg, J. *King and Kin.* Bloomington, IN: Indiana University Press, 1986.

Sack, R. D. *A Commentary on the Book of Genesis,* Lewiston: E. Mellen Press, 1990.

Sasson, J. "Numbers 5 and the Waters of Judgment," *Biblische Zeitschrift* 16 (1972) 249-251.

Schafer, P. and H. G. Kippenberg, *Envisioning Magic. A Princeton Seminar and Symposium.* Leiden: Brill, 1997.

_____. "Magic and Religion in Ancient Judaism," *Envisioning Magic. A Princeton Seminar and Symposium.* Eds. P. Schafer and H. G. Kippenberg. Leiden: Brill, 1997.

Scurlock, J. A. *Magical Means of Dealing with Ghosts in Ancient Mesopotamia.* Dissertation: University of Chicago, 1988.

_____. "Magic: Ancient Near East," in *The Anchor Bible Dictionary.* New York: Doubleday, 1992.

Segal, A. F. "Hellenistic Magic: Some Questions of Definition," *Studies in Gnosticism and Hellenistic Religions.* Eds. R. Van der Broek and M. J. Vermaseren. Leiden: Brill, 1981, 349-375.

Segal, J. B. "Popular Religion in Ancient Israel," *Journal of Jewish Studies* 27 (1976).

Seidel, J. "Charming Criminals: Classification of Magic in the Babylonian Talmud," *Ancient Magic and Ritual Power.* Eds. M. Meyer and P. Mirecki. Leiden: Brill, 1995, pp. 145-166.

_____. *Studies in Ancient Jewish Magic.* Dissertation: UC Berkeley, 1996.

Smith, J. Z. "Trading Places." *Ancient Magic and Ritual Power.* Eds. M. Meyer and P. Mirecki. Leiden: Brill, 1995, pp. 13-27.

_____. *Imagining Religion: From Babylon to Jonestown.* Chicago: University of Chicago Press, 1982.

_____. *Map is Not Territory. Studies in the History of Religions.* Leiden: Brill, 1978.

Smith, M. *Jesus the Magician.* San Francisco: Harper & Row, 1978.

Smith, T. "Clementine Recognitions" 3.57. *The Ante-Nicene Fathers*, vol. 8. New York: Charles Scribner's Sons, 1903.

Smith, W. Robertson. "On the Forms of Divination and Magic Enumerated in Deut 18:10-11." *Journal of Philology* 14 (1885): 112-128.

_____. "On the Forms of Divination and Magic Enumerated in Deut 18:10-11." *Journal of Philology* 13 (1884): 273-287.

_____. *Lectures on the Religion of the Semites*, 1884. Reprint, New York: Ktav 1969.

Snoek, J. A. M. *Initiations. A Methodological Approach to the Application of Classification and Definition Theory in the Study of Rituals.* Dissertation: Leiden 1987.

Sperber, D. *Magic and Folklore in Rabbinic Literature.* Tel Aviv: Bar Ilan University Press, 1994.

Stade "Beitraege zur Pentateuchkritik," sec. 3, "Die Eiferopferthora," *ZAW* 15 (1895), pp. 166-75.

Swartz, M. D. *Scholastic Magic: Ritual and Revelation in Early Jewish Mysticism.* Princeton University Press, 1996.

Tallquist, K. "Sumerisch-akkadische Hymnen der Totenwelt," *Studia Orientalia* 4 (1934), 17-22.

Tambiah, S. J. *Magic, Science, Religion and the Scope of Rationality*, Cambridge University Press, 1990.

Tawil, H. "Azazel the Prince of the Steppe: A Comparative Study," *ZAW* 92 (1980), 43-59.

Thomas, K. *Religion and the Decline of Magic.* New York: Charles Scribner's Sons, 1971.

Thompson, R. C. *Semitic Magic.* New York: Ktav Publishing House, 1971 (reprint of 1908).

Thompson, R. J. *Penitence and Sacrifice in Early Israel outside the Levitical Law.* Leiden: Brill, 1963.

Titiev, M. "A Fresh Approach to the Problem of Magic and Religion," *Southwestern Journal of Anthropology* 16 (1960) 292-98.

Tylor, E. B. *Primitive Culture: Researches into the Development of Mythology, Philosophy, Religion, Art and Custom.* London: John Murray, 1873.

Urbrock, W. J. "Blessings and Curses." *The Anchor Bible Dictionary.* Ed. D.N. Freedman. New York: Doubleday, 1992.

Van Beek, W. E. A. "The Religion of Everyday Life: An Ethnoscience Investigation into the Concepts of Religion and Magic," in *Explorations in the Anthropology of Religion.* Eds. W. E. A. Van Beek and J. H. Scherer. The Hague 1975, pp. 55-69.

Van der Toorn, K. "Ordeal." *The Anchor Bible Dictionary.* New York: Doubleday, 1992.

_____. "The Nature of Biblical Teraphim in the Light of Cuneiform Evidence." *Catholic Biblical Quarterly* 52 (1990).

Vaux, R. de. *Studies in Old Testament Sacrifice*. Cardiff: University of Wales Press, 1964.

Vergote, J. "Joseph in Egypt." *Orientalia et Biblica Lovaniensia* 3 (1959) 66-73.

Versnel, H. S. "Some Reflections on the Relationship Magic-Religion," *Numen* 38 (1991) 177-197.

Von Rad, G. *Deuteronomy*. Trans. D. Barton. Philadelphia: Westminster Press, 1973.

_____. *Genesis: A Commentary*. Trans. John H. Marks. Philadelphia: Westminster Press, 1972.

_____. *Old Testament Theology*, vol. 1, trans. D. M. G. Stalker. Edinburgh/London: Oliver and Boyd, 1962.

Walsh, J. T. *1 Kings*. Minneapolis: Liturgical Press, 1996.

Wax, M., and R. Wax, "The Notion of Magic," *Current Anthropology* 4 (1963) 495-518.

Weinfeld, M. "Deuteronomy, Book of," *The Anchor Bible Dictionary*. New York: Doubleday, 1992.

_____. "Burning Babies in Ancient Israel," *UF* 10 (1978): 411-413.

_____. "The Worship of Molech and of the Queen of Heaven and its Background," *UF* 4 (1972): 133-158.

_____. "The Covenant of Grant in the Old Testament and in the Ancient Near East," *JAOS* 90 (1970): 184-203.

_____. "The Extent of the Promised Land—The Status of Transjordan," in *Das Land Israel in biblischer Zeit*. Ed. G. Strecker. Gottingen,1983, pp. 59–75.

Westermann, C. *Blessing in the Bible and the Life of the Church*. Trans. K. Crim. Philadelphia: Fortress Press, 1978.

Wilson, R. R. *Prophecy and Society in Ancient Israel*. Philadelphia: Fortress Press, 1980.

Winkelman, M. J. *Shamans, Priests and Witches: A Cross-Cultural Study of Magico-Religious Practitioners*. Arizona State University Anthropological Research Papers No. 44: 1992.

_____. *Shamanism: The Neural Ecology of Consciousness and Healing*. Connecticut: Bergin and Garvey, 2000.

Wiseman, D. J. "Abban and Alalaḫ" *Journal of Cuneiform Studies* 12: 124–29.

Wittgenstein, L. *Philosophical Investigations*. Oxford: Blackwell, 1958.

Wright, D. P. *The Disposal of Impurity: Elimination Rites in the Bible and in Hittite and Mesopotamian Literature*. Atlanta: Scholars Press, 1987.

_____. "The Gesture of Hand Placement in the Hebrew Bible and in Hittite Literature," *JAOS* 106 (1986): 433-446.

Wright, G. E. "The Lawsuit of God: A Form-Critical Study of Deuteronomy 32," *Israel's Prophetic Heritage*. Eds. B. Anderson and W. Harrelson. New York: Harper, 1962.

Yahuda, A. S. *The Language of the Pentateuch in Its Relation to Egyptian*. London: Oxford University Press, 1933.

Zakovitch, Y. "Assimilation in Biblical Narratives," in *Empirical Models for Biblical Criticism.* Ed. J. Tigay. Philadelphia: University of Pennsylvania Press, 1985, pp. 185-92.

green
press
INITIATIVE

Eisenbrauns is committed to preserving ancient forests and natural resources. We elected to print this title on 30% post consumer recycled paper, processed chlorine free. As a result, for this printing, we have saved:

1 Trees (40' tall and 6-8" diameter)
381 Gallons of Wastewater
1 million BTU's of Total Energy
49 Pounds of Solid Waste
92 Pounds of Greenhouse Gases

Eisenbrauns made this paper choice because our printer, Thomson-Shore, Inc., is a member of Green Press Initiative, a nonprofit program dedicated to supporting authors, publishers, and suppliers in their efforts to reduce their use of fiber obtained from endangered forests.

For more information, visit www.greenpressinitiative.org

Environmental impact estimates were made using the Environmental Defense Paper Calculator. For more information visit: www.papercalculator.org.